"The apostle Paul said that the gosp[el] [was a stum]bling block to the Jews. The gospel [is offensive] or to use Greg Beale's term, *ironic*. To encounter [it is] strong evidence of the gospel's divinity. Beale does a masterful job of directing us to a powerful internal testimony the Scripture gives of its truthfulness. Furthermore, *Redemptive Reversals* is overflowing with anecdotal illustrations, pastoral cautions, cultural connections, and practical applications. It's a refreshing, unique, and important book all serious Bible students should have in their library."

J. D. Greear, President, Southern Baptist Convention; author, *Not God Enough*; Pastor, The Summit Church, Raleigh-Durham, North Carolina

"Greg Beale is one of the most perceptive and fascinating New Testament scholars of our day. He reads texts in their historical context, but he also illustrates how particular verses and passages fit into the larger storyline of the Scriptures. In this wonderfully accessible volume, Beale helps us to see that God often works in ways that we would not expect and uses unlikely and ironic means to accomplish his purposes. We see from Beale's work that God is sovereignly working out his purposes and his will and that we can trust him with our lives."

Thomas R. Schreiner, James Buchanan Harrison Professor of New Testament Interpretation, the Southern Baptist Theological Seminary

"An extraordinary book. It lays out a deeply biblical understanding of how God has reversed sin in Christ and how he judges sin in the world, sometimes in surprising ways. With its acute insights and unique perspective, it is a very helpful study."

David F. Wells, Senior Distinguished Research Professor of Theology, Gordon-Conwell Theological Seminary

"This book opened my eyes to look for the consistent way that God works ironically throughout the Bible—the way he punishes sinners by means of their own sin, makes life possible through his own death, shows his strength through our weakness, and exalts those who are humbled."

Nancy Guthrie, author, *Even Better than Eden: Nine Ways the Bible's Story Changes Everything about Your Story*

*Redemptive Reversals and the Ironic
Overturning of Human Wisdom*

Short Studies in Biblical Theology

Edited by Dane C. Ortlund and Miles V. Van Pelt

Redemptive Reversals and the Ironic Overturning of Human Wisdom

G. K. Beale

WHEATON, ILLINOIS

Trade paperback ISBN: 978-1-4335-6328-7
ePub ISBN: 978-1-4335-6331-7
PDF ISBN: 978-1-4335-6329-4
Mobipocket ISBN: 978-1-4335-6330-0

Library of Congress Cataloging-in-Publication Data

Names: Beale, G. K. (Gregory K.), 1949- author.
Title: Redemptive reversals and the ironic overturning of human wisdom / G.K. Beale.
Description: Wheaton : Crossway, 2019. | Series: Short studies in biblical theology | Includes bibliographical references and index.
Identifiers: LCCN 2019009166 (print) | LCCN 2019022067 (ebook) | ISBN 9781433563294 (pdf) | ISBN 9781433563300 (mobi) | ISBN 9781433563317 (epub) | ISBN 9781433563287 (tp)
Subjects: LCSH: Redemption–Christianity. | Irony. | Irony in the Bible. | Christianity. | Theology.
Classification: LCC BT775 (ebook) | LCC BT775 .B37 2019 (print) | DDC 234/.3–dc23
LC record available at https://lccn.loc.gov/2019009166

Crossway is a publishing ministry of Good News Publishers.

BP		29	28	27	26	25	24	23	22	21	20	19
15	14	13	12	11	10	9	8	7	6	5	4	3	2	1

To Lynn, Frank, and Helen Garrott,
pilgrims who have walked the ironic cruciform path of our Lord

Contents

Foreword

A Most Unlikely Revival

I asked my longtime friend Andrew White to write a foreword. Andrew is a medical doctor and former student of mine from when I taught at Gordon-Conwell Theological Seminary. He is an excellent doctor and perceptive theologian. The true story he tells here exemplifies many of the ideas in this book.

My story is thirty-seven years old, yet every time I tell it (which is often), my listeners encourage me to tell it to more people, using mass media. Greg Beale and his wife, Dorinda, have been the most persistent and persuasive listeners. So I am finally putting to pen a personal, historical account of a spiritual revival in 1980 among the Khmer Rouge in a refugee camp at the Thailand/Cambodia border called Sa Kaeo. This story is amazing because a revival was so unlikely for two reasons: (1) The Khmer Rouge (many of whom were converted in the revival) had been vicious murderers in the Cambodian genocide of the 1970s. That genocide had a greater percentage of the population killed than in any other genocide in the history of the world. (2) Those who spearheaded the revival were the most unlikely people at best—a murderer, an over-the-hill missionary, and a severely depressed doctor. In spite of these two serious problems, a wonderful revival was clearly authored by God, and it brought him great glory.

In order to set the stage for this true story, I must give you a brief history of Cambodia from 1975 to 1979 (the period of time detailed in the award-winning movie *The Killing Fields*). My main source for this history is from the website *Cambodian Tribunal Monitor*.[1] The Khmer (Cambodian) Rouge (Red), otherwise known as the Communist Party of Kampuchea, ruled Cambodia from 1975 to 1979. The Khmer Rouge leader, Pol Pot, took control of Cambodia in 1975 in the wake of a civil war that ousted Prince Sihanouk. Pol Pot wanted to transform Cambodia into a rural, classless society not unlike communist China. People were not allowed to leave their rural cooperatives, and if three or more people gathered together in unapproved conversation, they risked being charged as enemies of the state and executed. Others worked twelve hours a day, and many died from inadequate rest, starvation, and lack of medical services. Cambodian soldiers, military officers, and civil servants under Prince Sihanouk, as well as intellectuals, city residents, and minority groups, were detained, interrogated, imprisoned, tortured, and executed.

Many who escaped execution were members of Prince Sihanouk's Free Khmer, who fought against the Khmer Rouge. For the most part, the Free Khmer were overpowered by the Khmer Rouge. Many of the Free Khmer fled into neighboring Thailand. When the Vietnamese fought their way into Cambodia to conquer it in 1979, the Khmer Rouge had killed nearly two million of its own people. In

---

1. http://www.cambodiatribunal.org/history/cambodian-history/khmer-rouge-history/.

the wake of the Vietnamese offensive, the Khmer Rouge, like the Free Khmer, fled into neighboring Thailand. For obvious reasons, the Khmer Rouge and Free Khmer were housed in different refugee camps. One of the Khmer Rouge refugee camps at the Thailand/Cambodia border was Sa Kaoe, where I served as the attending physician on a malaria ward for just two weeks in the spring of 1980. But I am getting ahead of my story.

I was a resident physician in family medicine in Charleston, South Carolina, from 1978 to 1981. My wife and I heard of the genocide in Cambodia at a church service in the winter of 1979, and on our way home from that service, I told my wife that I would really like to help the Free Khmer refugees. That was not possible, however, because I could not be released from my duties as a second-year family medicine resident. My wife and I decided that at least we could pray for the refugees.

When I went to the residency center the following day, I found a remarkable memo in my mailbox. The memo, from the dean of the medical university of South Carolina, said that in response to the refugee crisis in Cambodia, resident physicians could be released from their duties to serve in Cambodia and that the service would be credited to their diplomas. Additionally, all service provided would be financed by the Southern Baptist Church. I immediately called my wife and told her that I had received a handwritten message from God. I could hardly tell God no to what couldn't have been a clearer calling. Even though we had a six-month-old son, my wife fully supported my decision to help in this potentially dangerous mission.

In preparation for our departure to Cambodia, a group of Charleston resident physicians and faculty from many different medical disciplines met together regularly to plan our mission and create a strong support group. By the spring of 1980 we had bonded and were ready to fly to Thailand. However, when I stepped off the plane in Thailand, I had a panic attack, which rapidly precipitated a severe depression. I have had a history of severe depressions since the age of ten (seven depressions in all, with the seventh lasting thirteen years). I experience depression as terror, searing mental pain, poor concentration, inaccessible memory, mental exhaustion, a seeming inability to do even the smallest tasks, and a longing for death. Needless to say I could not understand why God allowed me to become so depressed when I had been so excited about my six-week mission to the Cambodians in Thailand.

I was initially assigned to a mission hospital in Thailand, for two weeks, to be initiated into the Thailand culture and local medical practice. Fortunately I found some imipramine (an antidepressant) in the mission pharmacy. Unfortunately it takes four to six weeks for the antidepressant to take effect. So despite the medicine, I remained severely depressed. After two weeks I was transferred back to my mission team at a camp for the Free Khmer. When I arrived at the Free Khmer refugee camp, I found that there were too many physicians for the number of refugees, and I was left with nothing to do. With this new reality, I became even more depressed since I couldn't understand why God had sent me to Thailand if there was no need for my medical services. After two weeks of doing almost nothing except drowning in my depression, our mission group received a memo from Sa Kaeo, a Khmer Rouge refugee camp in northeastern Thailand. The memo said Sa Kaeo was in need of a physician for a malaria ward, since the attending physician had become ill and had to return to the United States. No one in our mission team wanted the assignment because we were such a cohesive group. I, however, experienced a remarkably clear sense from God that I needed to accept the assignment. I knew that from a mental health perspective, leaving my support group was the worst possible choice, but somehow I knew that God would take care of me. I also knew that

God would help me get over my well-founded prejudice against the murderous Khmer Rouge.

When I arrived at the Khmer Rouge refugee camp in Sa Kaeo, I was assigned to a malaria ward. Upon being admitted to the medical ward, most patients were too ill to talk to, apart from their medical history. By the second day, however, most were more attentive. God had impressed upon me that I needed to share the gospel with every patient through an interpreter. I was, however, so depressed that the only thing I could communicate was to ask all the patients whether there was sin in their lives. The response was uniformly yes. Given the recent history of the Khmer Rouge, it is not surprising that so many would recognize their sin. Still, I was amazed at the honesty of 100 percent of my patients, and I then told them that I would bring good news about their sin the next day.

As I made ward rounds the following day, many of the patients had big smiles on their faces. They told me they had not been able to wait to hear the good news from me and so had sought out the ward chaplain. The chaplain was a retired Cambodian Methodist mission-ary. He had had only a small harvest of faithful believers while he was in Cambodia, but he could speak Cambodian fluently and had translated the biblical book of John into Khmer (Cambodian). The missionary chaplain lacked a charismatic personality, but he clearly loved Jesus and was a channel of the Holy Spirit.

There was only one Khmer Rouge patient on my ward who could read. In Cambodia he had been a vicious leader. Somehow, he had escaped death—the majority of those who could read had been killed because they were considered intellectuals. He was very ill, suffering with the most fatal form of malaria, complicated by bacterial pneu-monia. His chest X-ray hung over his bed on a clothesline for easy viewing. During the day when this patient felt stronger (a strength I felt was miraculous, given the severity of his illnesses), he stood up on his cot and read aloud in a strong voice from the beginning to the end of John, over and over again. Periodically he would point to the abnormality on his chest X-ray and tell his fellow patients that God was healing him of the pneumonia. While he read, the Holy Spirit was a palpable reality throughout the ward.

When I made rounds the second day, I very briefly shared the good news to those who were not smiling. I simply told them that Jesus Christ had died for their sins, and if they trusted him, they would be completely forgiven. A full half of them accepted Jesus as Savior and Lord. The missionary chaplain had to explain to them in more detail the meaning and necessity of salvation. I was too depressed to do that. Two of my patients died but not before they favorably received the good news of Jesus, the forgiver of their sin and the joy of their salvation.

Also remarkable was that God was rapidly raising up a Khmer Rouge evangelist who had been discipled by our missionary chaplain. He had been a Christian for only three weeks. The evangelist was no Billy Graham, but daily he went to the scores of new house churches in the camp (which were really just shacks). There he evangelized and discipled the Cambodians all day at great risk of martyrdom at the hand of the unconverted Khmer Rouge leaders. Those who were part of the house churches were also at great risk. The Khmer Rouge leaders told the people that if they converted to Christianity, they would have to "lay on the ground" when they returned to Cambodia, a euphemism for digging your own grave. At the end of each day the evangelist was exhausted but was unable to sleep and was visibly trembling from anxiety. Each night I would give him a shot of Valium (a tranquilizer and sleep medicine). Each morning he woke up refreshed and continued his vigorous ministry.

I was at Sa Kaeo for only two weeks but participated in a spiritual revival that ultimately led to the salvation of several thousand Khmer

Rouge refugees. I heard some time after I left Sa Kaeo that the new Christian refugees asked the Thailand government to allow them to build a Christian church. Thailand is predominantly Buddhist, so the government told the Christian refugees that they could not build a church until there was a Buddhist temple. Seeking the Lord's guidance, the Christian Khmer Rouge first built a Buddhist temple, which was hardly used, and then a large, thriving Christian church.

As I began this story I recounted the two reasons a revival was so unlikely at Sa Kaeo. First, the converts were among the vilest and most hardened sinners the world has ever known (every bit as evil as the Nazi SS). Second, the leaders of the revival were the least suitable people for participation in a revival. The four leaders of the revival whom God had raised up were (1) a severely depressed doctor (me) of a busy malarial ward who was mentally capable only of sharing the most elementary gospel message; (2) a retired missionary minister who had seen little fruit while serving in Cambodia but knew Cambodian and had translated John; (3) an exhausted, anxious, brand-new Khmer Rouge evangelist; and (4) a rare Khmer Rouge patient who could read and was sick with the most fatal form of malaria, complicated by pneumonia. Nevertheless, he read the Gospel of John over and over again.

These four weak vessels were used by the Lord in an astounding way. During the time I was in Thailand, I had no joy despite the many conversions I witnessed, because I was so depressed. But now I am full of great joy thinking about the way the Lord used weak vessels, including me, in order to maximize his glory. Jesus clearly led this great revival, leaving no doubt that the Holy Spirit was responsible for it.

I continue to have recurrent severe depressions, so I look forward to the day when my feeble mind is completely renewed in the eternal new creation. Even during my deepest depressions, however,

I can take some comfort in the way God used me in a Khmer Rouge revival in a refugee camp at the Thailand/Cambodia border in 1980. Over the years I have come to trust God increasingly. If God could use me when I was so severely depressed, how could I not trust him with all other things? God always brings glory to himself, and being a weak vessel is no obstacle to the accomplishment of his will—his good and perfect will.

My life is a testimony that God uses weakness to produce strength and thus accomplish his gracious rule. Indeed, Jesus said to the apostle Paul, "'My grace is sufficient for you, for my power is made perfect in weakness.' Therefore [Paul says] I will boast all the more gladly of my weaknesses so that the power of Christ may rest upon me. Therefore, I am content with weaknesses . . . with distresses . . . with calamities, for when I am weak, then I am strong" (2 Cor. 12:9–10). This is the irony of Christian living, upon which this book by my friend and former teacher, Greg Beale, will elaborate.

Andrew A. White, MD, MATS, 2017

Series Preface

Most of us tend to approach the Bible early on in our Christian lives as a vast, cavernous, and largely impenetrable book. We read the text piecemeal, finding golden nuggets of inspiration here and there, but remain unable to plug any given text meaningfully into the overarching storyline. Yet one of the great advances in evangelical biblical scholarship over the past few generations has been the recovery of biblical theology—that is, a renewed appreciation for the Bible as a theologically unified, historically rooted, progressively unfolding, and ultimately Christ-centered narrative of God's covenantal work in our world to redeem sinful humanity.

This renaissance of biblical theology is a blessing, yet little of it has been made available to the general Christian population. The purpose of Short Studies in Biblical Theology is to connect the resurgence of biblical theology at the academic level with everyday believers. Each volume is written by a capable scholar or churchman who is consciously writing in a way that requires no prerequisite theological training of the reader. Instead, any thoughtful Christian disciple can track with and benefit from these books.

Each volume in this series takes a whole-Bible theme and traces it through Scripture. In this way readers not only learn about a given theme but also are given a model for how to read the Bible as a coherent whole.

We have launched this series because we love the Bible, we love the church, and we long for the renewal of biblical theology in the academy to enliven the hearts and minds of Christ's disciples all around the world. As editors, we have found few discoveries more thrilling in life than that of seeing the whole Bible as a unified story of God's gracious acts of redemption, and indeed of seeing the whole Bible as ultimately about Jesus, as he himself testified (Luke 24:27; John 5:39).

The ultimate goal of Short Studies in Biblical Theology is to magnify the Savior and to build up his church—magnifying the Savior through showing how the whole Bible points to him and his gracious rescue of helpless sinners; and building up the church by strengthening believers in their grasp of these life-giving truths.

Dane C. Ortlund and Miles V. Van Pelt

Introduction

Our life consists of ups and downs. We are usually surprised by both, but we should not be so surprised, since the Bible testifies that such ups and downs are part of the divinely designed warp and woof of life. This is true of both the believer in Christ and the unbeliever. But what may appear for the unbeliever as a positive upturn in life is sometimes really, from God's view and plan, the beginning of a downturn in judgment. And what appears to be a downturn in the believer's life is really an upturn in blessing.

These ups and downs involve ironic patterns. What is *irony*? Irony is the saying of something or the doing of something that implies its opposite. What is said or done really indicates the reverse of the saying or act. This book is about the notion that God deals with humans in primarily ironic ways. The Bible is a record of how God has so dealt with humans. There are two kinds of biblical or theological irony. There is *retributive irony* whereby God punishes people by the very means of their own sin. We will see this in chapters 1 and 2. There is also *redemptive irony* whereby the faithful appear to be cursed, but as they persevere in faith, they are really in the midst of being blessed.[1] We will see this in chapters 3 to 6. Both kinds of

---

1. Warren Austin Gage first formulated these two kinds of theological irony in a personal conversation, which has helped me to clarify better these kinds of ironies in the Bible.

theological ironies are true of humans in general. Everyone is ultimately caught in the matrix of one of these two ironic patterns of living. Christians need to be aware of the ironic nature of life in order that they not become discouraged at bad events in their lives. In fact, we will see that the ironic nature of Christian living is necessary in order that faith be given opportunity to grow.

This book explains how Scripture depicts these two kinds of irony in the lives of people. And how these two ironies reach their zenith points in Satan (through retributive irony) and in Christ (through redemptive irony). As you read this book, you will perceive more of the nature of what irony is. Before I can discuss irony in the Scriptures, however, I must talk briefly about the various kinds of literary ironies.[2]

At its core, "irony is saying one thing and meaning another."[3] All ironies are composed of three basic elements: (1) two or more layers or levels of meaning (one to the observer and one to the victim). (2) One layer has an opposite meaning to that of the other layer (respectively, what is apparent is the opposite of what is reality). (3) Either the observer or the victim is unaware of this tension or surprised by it.[4] Generally, three kinds of ironies have traditionally been recognized in literary studies. There is *verbal irony*, which is saying one thing and meaning its opposite. Here a verbal statement is aimed at a particular person. Second, there is *dramatic irony* or an irony of narrated events, wherein narrated events are turned to the opposite of the way that they appeared to be heading. Finally, there is *character irony*, part of dramatic irony, whereby one's true character stands in contrast with what he appears to be.[5]

---

2. I am grateful to my research assistant, Tyler Milliken, for his research into literary irony, of which the brief remainder of this chapter is a summary.

3. Jerry Camery-Hoggatt, *Irony in Mark's Gospel: Text and Subtext* (New York: Cambridge University Press, 1992), 60, citing Cicero.

4. Camery-Hoggatt, *Irony in Mark's Gospel*, 61, citing D. C. Muecke, *The Compass of Irony*, 1st ed. (London: Methuen Young, 1969), 19–20.

5. See InHee C. Berg, *Irony in the Matthean Passion Narrative* (Minneapolis: Fortress, 2014), 79–80, 88, 95, for discussion of these three ironies.

Luke's narrative of the rejection of the gospel by the Jews is satu-
rated with irony. In particular, Luke's narration of the rejection of
Jesus is mirrored by the depiction in Acts, where every effort to stand
against God's plan only fulfills it in every prophetic detail (e.g., see
Acts 2:23 and 13:27). In Luke, the rejection of Jesus by the Jews is
the catalyst for his redeeming death, whereas in Acts the persecution of the church becomes the catalyst for saving evangelism. Luke
also develops the principle that "some are last who will be first and
some are first who will be last" (Luke 13:30). These programmatic
ironies run throughout Luke-Acts.[6] Thus, some of the highest forms
of biblical irony are where there is narrated an "unexpected reversal
of fate and fortune," which is "the jolting turn of events" wherein "the
mighty are brought low and humble exalted."[7]

In John 19 the Roman soldiers mock the bleeding Jesus by saying their "Hail to the King!" The soldiers do not believe that Jesus
is any kind of king, and they intend their sarcastic words to be a
direct attack on Jesus, whom they believe is an imposter. A reader
perceives that the "lower" level of the mocking is false, whereas the
irony becomes apparent at the "higher" level, where it is evident that
the soldiers are the real victims of their own mocking, since they
are crucifying the one who is, in fact, the true divine king of the
universe.[8] Another example of this kind of irony is Paul's claim in
2 Corinthians 12:10: "When I am weak, then I am strong."[9]

So now we turn to the substance of the book.

---

6. E.g., see Jerry L. Ray, *Narrative Irony in Luke–Acts* (Lewiston, NY: Edwin Mellen Press,
1996), 109–11. For brief definition of dialectical irony (or programmatic irony), see p. 38; on
Acts 2:23, see pp. 109–10; on the negative consequences of Jewish rejection and positive Gentile
consequences in Acts 13:27–52, see pp. 110–11.

7. Paul Duke, *Irony in the Fourth Gospel* (Atlanta: John Knox Press, 1985), 11.

8. Cf. similarly on John 19:1–3 in Duke, *Irony in the Fourth Gospel*, 132.

9. Karl A. Plank, *Paul and the Irony of Affliction* (Atlanta: Scholars Press, 1987), 21n13.

1

God Judges People by
Their Own Sin

[The Nazi War criminal Josef] Mengele did not entirely escape
punishment. . . . The aging fugitive . . . "lived apprehensive and
afraid, fearful of being found by Jews." . . . He suffered migraine
headaches and slept with a Mauser pistol by his bed. . . . Though
there was never a punishment that would fit the dimensions of
Mengele's crimes, is it not peculiarly appropriate that he was
condemned to a lifetime of fearing his own victims, and that his
punishment should be inflicted by himself?

—Otto Fredrick, *Time*, June 24, 1985

One of my favorite pastimes in graduate school, after completing a big
paper or final exam, was to go to the local ice cream shop and reward
myself with a huge bowl of chocolate mint ice cream. This was the
height of culinary delight. In reality, I found many excuses to reward

myself with such treats. A few years later when I went to my doctor for a physical, he informed me that were I to continue over the years with this ice cream binge, my health would be seriously affected. I realized that the very thing in which I was finding great pleasure could at the same time be causing me, quite literally, "heartache" in the long run. But perhaps my biggest mistake was telling my wife what the doctor had said. I should have known that forever afterward, she would remind me of this sober truth. I have never been able to enjoy my huge bowls of chocolate mint ice cream since. Most of us are familiar with this kind of omnivorous irony. There are so many delicacies that do our taste buds good but simultaneously "do in" our bodies.

On a more serious note, punitive ironies transcend culinary bounds. There are many things people do purely for pleasure or self-interest even though they know it may hurt them in the long run.

A former student of mine, while taking a final exam on the subject of biblical ethics, tried to get a good grade by cheating. During the exam she approached me at the front of the room in order to get clarification about one of the questions. As she pointed her finger to the question on the exam paper, I saw answers written on her hand. The very way she attempted to succeed—through cheating—was the very way in which she failed.

From the political realm, many can probably recall the Machiavellian irony involving former President Richard Nixon. He attempted unjustly to become one of the most famous presidents in American history. He hoped to ensure his success by having all his conversations in the Oval Office recorded. Indeed, Nixon became our most infamous president because these very tapes exposed his underhanded attempts to defeat his political opponents.

These illustrations reflect an ironic moral principle, that when a person unethically schemes to succeed, often the scheme is discovered by the potential victims before it can be accomplished. The very way by which people attempt sinfully to get ahead often becomes the very means by which they fail.

This principle is at work in every level of life. An article in *Time* magazine some years ago made this observation about drugs: "People addicted to cocaine are out of control. . . . So it is a mean, symmetrical irony that cocaine's effect is to mimic will and emotional focus, permitting the user to feel he is blessed with precisely the virtues he lacks."[1] I know a woman who drank excessively so that she would feel less inhibited when she socialized. This appeared to work for awhile until she had to quit drinking permanently because of a liver ailment. In her later years, because of the deadening effects of alcohol, she had no personality but sat and stared blankly in the midst of social gatherings. The very things in which people wrongly attempt to find liberation frequently become the things that bring them into harsher bondage.

This ironic principle of judgment is expressed well in the proverb, "There is a way which seems right to man, but its end is the way of death" (Prov. 16:25). When we set out to succeed at something in an unethical manner, circumstances often have an uncanny way of reversing so that we are forced to fail.

In the light of what we have already discussed, we can define irony generally as the doing or saying of something that implies its opposite. What is done or said is really the reverse of what at first appears to be the case. God frequently deals with humanity in an ironic way. This is true in his acts of judgment and salvation, so that irony is one of the major thematic threads tying together the whole of Scripture. God repeatedly drives the events of history in the reverse direction from which they first appear to be moving. We look first at how God carries out his work of ironic punishment.

---

1. Kurt Andersen, "Crashing on Cocaine," *Time*, April 11, 1983, 25.

It's a Turn-Around World

There was once a Persian prince named Haman and a Jew of low status called Mordecai. Mordecai had saved the king of Persia by revealing a plot to kill the king, although the king was unaware that it was Mordecai who had made the plot known. Haman hated Mordecai because he would not bow down and pay homage to him as vice president of Persia (Est. 3:1–5). As a result, Haman vented his childish anger by persuading King Ahasuerus to decree that all Jews in the empire be annihilated (Est. 3:6–15), and he plotted to have Mordecai hanged on the gallows (Est. 5:14).

As providence would have it, the night before Mordecai was to be hanged, the king could not sleep, so he ordered his servants to read to him for pleasure's sake the recent records of the affairs of the kingdom. In these records the king heard it read that it was Mordecai who had revealed the assassination plot against him. Upon discovering that Mordecai had not been honored for this, he desired to make things right. Now at this very time Haman happened to be entering the king's court to request permission to hang Mordecai. Before Haman had the opportunity to discuss Mordecai, the king asked him, "What is to be done for the man whom the king desires to honor?" (Est. 6:6). Haman, thinking the king was referring to him, answered,

> For the man whom the king desires to honor, let them bring a royal robe which the king has worn, and the horse on which the king has ridden, and on whose head a royal crown has been placed; and let the robe and the horse be handed over to one of the king's noble princes and let them array the man whom the king desires to honor and lead him on horseback through the city square, and proclaim before him, "Thus it shall be done to the man whom the king desires to honor. (Est. 6:7–9)

Haman was shocked and humiliated when the king commanded him to "do so for Mordecai the Jew" (Est. 6:10), especially since Haman was required to lead Mordecai's horse through the city square. This was certainly an unexpected turn of events, but it was only the beginning of an even greater ironic reversal.

After the king had authorized Haman's plot (Est. 3:8–11), Queen Esther, Mordecai's step-daughter, informed the king about Haman's plot to exterminate all the Jews (which included Esther) and to hang Mordecai. The king angrily declared that Haman should be hanged on the very gallows upon which he had planned to hang Mordecai (Esther 7), and he made it possible for the Jews throughout his land to destroy Haman's allies who were planning to exterminate them (Esther 8–9). Therefore, "when the enemies of the Jews hoped to gain the mastery over them, it was turned to the contrary so that the Jews themselves gained the mastery" (Est. 9:1), and "it was a month which was turned for them from sorrow into gladness" (Est. 9:22). The Lord had designed that Haman's wicked scheme "which he had devised . . . should return on his own head" (Est. 9:25). That the name "Haman" in Hebrew may mean "celebrated one" is likely not coincidence. He tried to win a victory over the Jews and celebrate, but he was the one defeated and celebrated over by his enemies (Est. 9:17–22, 27). In fact, this victory has been celebrated by the Jews as the festival of Purim for centuries ever since.

Surely the story of Mordecai's rise and Haman's demise exemplifies a more general principle whereby God "sets on high those who are lowly, and those who mourn are lifted to safety," but "He frustrates the plotting of the shrewd, so that their hands cannot attain success" (Job 5:11–12), for "his own scheme brings him down. . . . And . . . a noose for him is hidden in the ground" (Job 18:7–10).

An Eye for an Eye

This story from the book of Esther is illustrative of the same idea found repeatedly in the Old Testament, where God punishes sinners by means of their own sin. The principle of ironic justice is lucidly summarized in Leviticus 24:19–31:

> If a man injures his neighbor, just as he has done, so shall it be done to him: fracture for fracture, eye for eye . . . just as he has injured a man, so it shall be inflicted on him. (cf. Ex. 21:23–25)

The idea is that the form of a man's punishment is to be patterned after the form of his crime or sin.[2] So, for example, the very act of killing another shows the pattern of how the killer must be punished— he must also be killed. Hence, killing may seem the right way to act for a man, but its end is the way of death. Furthermore, the murderer will be punished by means of his own sin.

That this is not an atypical form of divine punishment is born out by the Psalms:

> Hold them guilty, O God;
> By their own devices let them fall! (Ps. 5:10)

> [The wicked man] has dug a pit and hollowed it out,
> And he has fallen into the hole which he made.
> His mischief will return upon his own head. (Ps. 7:15–16)

Speaking of the judgment of evil nations, David says: "In the net which they hid, their own foot has been caught. The LORD

---

2. Exodus 21:23–25 is known as the *lex talionis* (law of retaliation) in which the punishment resembles the crime committed. Strictly speaking, this principle is literally true *primarily* in the case of murder. Otherwise Exodus 21 becomes a figurative expression to denote that the gravity of punishment must be equal to the gravity of the crime. But we shall see that the literal understanding is observable throughout the Old Testament.

has . . . executed judgment. In the work of his own hands the wicked is snared" (Ps. 9:15–16). Perhaps reflecting on the times when Saul was hunting David with the sword, David asserts, "The wicked have drawn the sword . . . to slay those who are upright in conduct. Their sword will enter their own heart" (Ps. 37:14–15; cf. 1 Sam. 31:4). In light of this, the verdict of ironic justice upon Saul was predictable, as he took his life by falling on his own sword (1 Sam. 31:4). Likewise, David's son Solomon states, "He who rolls a stone, it will come back on him" (Prov. 26:27). Indeed, "there is a way which seems right to a man, but its end is the way of death" (Prov. 14:12; 16:25). In the Old Testament this ironic principle of justice was most observed by the "wise man" who discerned its repeated occurrence in the lives of others (see Job 18:8; Pss. 35:8; 57:6; 64:3–8; 75:4–5, 10; 115:2–8; Prov. 1:18–19, 31; 14:32; 21:7, 13; 22:16; 26:27; 28:10, 22).

You Shall Reap What You Sow

Is it a coincidence that most of the statements of ironic judgment are found in the wisdom writings of the psalmist of Israel, David? It is likely no accident, since David, perhaps more than any man of his time, had experienced God's ironic judgment upon himself. However, that he so often records the principle is a demonstration that he learned from it with a repentant attitude. But what was this judgment upon David, and what had he done to deserve it? Second Samuel 12:9–11 summarizes the sin and judgment:

> You have struck down Uriah the Hittite with the sword, have taken his wife to be your wife. . . . Now therefore, the sword shall never depart from your house. . . . I will even take your wives before your eyes and give them to your companion, and he will lie with your wives in broad daylight.

Surely David was being punished by means of the very sins that he had committed. David's murder of Uriah by the sword was punished by his sons Amnon and Absalom being likewise murdered (cf. 2 Sam. 13; 18). And just as David committed adultery with another's wife, so his wives became similarly abused (2 Sam. 16:22). David should not have been surprised by the severity of this ironic penalty, since he would have remembered a similar fate by another king during his youth. Perhaps the verdict pronounced by Nathan the prophet echoed in David's mind the sentence passed on Agag, king of the Amalekites, by Samuel the prophet: "'As your sword has made women childless, so shall your mother be childless among women.' And Samuel hewed Agag to pieces before the LORD at Gilgal" (1 Sam. 15:33). The ironic judgment of Saul must have been evident even before his suicide: "Because you [Saul] have rejected the word of the LORD, He [God] has also rejected you from being king" (1 Sam. 15:23). And, of course, the suicidal end of Saul's life should have been clearer in mind. Nevertheless, as we will see, David's own life is spared, and his curse is turned ultimately into a blessing because of his repentant spirit.

David's case is instructive, since it shows that even believers in the Lord "reap what they sow." Their punishment may not have the eternal dimension as with the unbeliever, but it is nonetheless real. Just as Jacob the believer deceived his father Isaac through wearing the skins of goats and masquerading himself as Esau, so Jacob was deceived by his sons when they masqueraded Joseph's death by sprinkling goat's blood on Joseph's tunic. Arthur Pink has well said:

> Though God forgives His people their sins, yet He frequently gives them plain proof of His holy abhorrence of the same, and causes them to taste something of the bitter fruits which they bring forth.[3]

---

3. A. W. Pink, *The Life of David*, vol. 2 (Swengel, PA: Reiner, 1976), 24.

Christians should well consider their actions and the possible consequences. How many Christian young people desire to be married? Yet the primary qualities sought in a potential mate are often attractive appearance and personality. Spiritual motivations and commitment to the Lord are too often overlooked. When a Christian marries a non-Christian troubles are bound to come. The unbeliever cannot understand the spiritual zeal of his Christian mate. Consequently, the unbelieving mate reacts antagonistically to spiritual activities such as family devotions, mealtime prayer, and church attendance. This reaction is inevitable because of the non-Christian mate's exclusive focus on the physical realm.

The point is that when Christians emphasize external realities when choosing a spouse, this choice can be the very thing that curses them later. The very things wrongly viewed as blessings at the beginning ironically become the very things that plague and thwart the attempted spiritual growth of Christians. This can affect the children of such marriages as well! Solomon's pursuit of sexual and political indulgence with an abundance of wives likewise came back to haunt him, for it was this very thing that "turned his heart away after other gods" (1 Kings 11:4). How ironic that the author of the ideal marriage relationship (Song of Solomon) did not heed his own lessons. Like his father, David, Solomon, too, later realized the futility of his sin (cf. Eccles. 2:8–11). In so many ways, we can be judged by the very things we want to think are right but are really sinful. "There is a way which seems right to a man, but its end is the way of death" (Prov. 14:12).

Your Sins Will Find You Out

Although God's people are viewed as suffering under his chastening hand, the ironic judgment of unbelievers receives much description in the Bible, especially those who represent the kingdom of Satan. With such people in mind, David proclaims in Psalm 10:2, "In pride the wicked hotly pursue the afflicted; let them be caught in the plots which they have devised." Again and again throughout Scripture the wicked are seen as either oppressing God's people or attempting to kill them in order to receive some earthly reward. And just as often, their efforts to overcome the godly backfire on them, much as is portrayed in *The Road Runner Show* cartoons where the coyote always becomes frustrated by trapping himself in the trap he has laid for the road runner (indeed, "He who rolls a stone, it will come back on him," Prov. 26:27).

Traitors Betray Themselves

It is likely that the ironic patterns of life were further impressed on David's mind because of events that transpired in the latter part of his reign. It was tragically after David had just forgiven Absalom his son for murdering another son, Amnon, that Absalom repaid the kindness by leading a rebellion to overthrow David (2 Sam. 15–20). To add to David's troubles, his best friend and trusted counselor, Ahithophel, sided with Absalom in the conspiracy. Absalom's only motive was self-aggrandizement—he wanted to be king—but Ahithophel was probably seeking revenge against David for his murder of Uriah and adultery with Bathsheba, the granddaughter of Ahithophel. However, when Ahithophel's strategy for assassinating David was mysteriously rejected by Absalom, Ahithophel committed suicide (2 Sam. 16:20–17:14, 23). He knew if his plan were not followed, the rebellion would not succeed. Ahithophel was right. Absalom followed another plan of attack and was killed in battle.

Absalom was the most handsome man in Israel, especially because of his beautiful hair. Since he took such pride in his beautiful head of hair, he cut it only once every year (2 Sam. 14:25–26). Yet it was because of his "heavy head of hair" (14:26) that he met his end. As he was riding through a forest during the battle, "his head caught fast in the oak, so he was left hanging" until he was found and killed by David's army (2 Sam. 18:9–15). The source of his pride brought about his downfall. Absalom, whose name in Hebrew means "Father of Peace," was just the opposite—a son of contention. Truly "the advice of the cunning is quickly thwarted" (Job 5:13). Absalom and Ahithophel attempted unjustly to kill David, but before they could succeed, their plot was turned back on their own head. The very means by which they hoped to dispose of David was the very way by which they were disposed of. The following words penned by David may well have this evil duo in mind:

> For without cause they hid their net for me;
> Without cause they dug a pit for my soul. . . .
> Let the net which he hid catch himself;
> Into that very destruction let him fall. (Ps. 35:7–8)

A Preincarnate Hitler

The pharaoh of ancient Egypt is one of the best examples of ironic judgment, since in great arrogance he hotly pursued afflicted Israel but was "caught in the plots which [he had] devised" (Ps. 10:2). Pharaoh's first mistake was to claim to be God. He gave to himself such titles as "savior of Egypt," "Lord of the living," "Universal god," and the sovereign "god of heaven and earth." As such he was also held to be the divine judge after death.[4] This is, no doubt, why Pharaoh responds to Moses's message that begins, "Thus says the LORD" (Ex. 5:1), with an equally authoritative, "Thus says Pharaoh" (Ex. 5:10). But, indeed, such a divine claim was farthest from the truth since,

---

4. For a background of Pharaoh's divine names and functions consult I. Engnell, *Studies in Divine Kingship in the Ancient Near East* (Oxford, UK: Blackwell, 1967); S. Morenz, *Egyptian Religion* (Ithaca, NY: Cornell University Press, 1960); E. L. R. Meyerowitz, *The Divine Kingship in Ghana and Ancient Egypt* (London: Faber & Faber, 1960); H. Frankfort, *Kingship and the Gods* (Chicago: University of Chicago Press, 1948).

ironically, Scripture identifies the pharaoh of the exodus with Satan, "the dragon" (Isa. 51:9; cf. Ps. 74:13–14 and Rev. 12:3–4, 7–9), and the "sea monster" (Ps. 89:10; cf. also Ps. 87:4; Isa. 30:7; Ezek. 32:2). Pharaoh's obstinate claim to deity, even in spite of the plagues that came upon him in Exodus 7–13, was the reason for his judgment.

Pharaoh's mistaken belief in his divine sovereignty must have led him to issue the edict that the firstborn males of Israel were to be killed by the Hebrew midwives (Ex. 1:16), and when this failed, he ordered the firstborn to be drowned in a river (Ex. 1:22). Not only did Pharaoh's attempts to overcome Israel fail, but his edicts declaring the killing of the firstborn were providentially reversed so that they fell on him in judgment. Not only did God kill the firstborn of every Egyptian family (Ex. 12:29), but he also drowned Pharaoh's army in the Red Sea (Ex. 15:1–12). His sins came back on his own head, since he was punished ironically by the very things he perpetrated against Israel.

No Truth and No Consequences

Before we leave this discussion of Pharaoh, it is further enlightening to understand his role as the purported savior of those who died and faced imminent judgment. The Egyptians believed that after death, people had to go through a trial in the Hall of Judgment to determine whether they were guilty of earthly sin. If found innocent, a person inherited eternal bliss, but if found guilty, he or she suffered judgment. There were two parts to this judgment process. (1) The deceased person arrived at one end of the Hall of Judgment and was presented with a long list of sins characteristic of human life, which he or she categorically denied. (2) While the denial of sin was taking place, the deceased's heart was being weighed on the "scales of judgment" at the other end of the hall in order to see if its testimony supported the person's denial. The Egyptians believed that all people are sinful and that the heart would tell the truth if it were separated from the bad influence of the body, so when the heart confessed the deceased's sins, it would become "heavy" with sin, and the disequilibrium of the scales would indicate guilt and judgment. Therefore, the heart's confession of sin would demonstrate that the deceased's denial was a lie, with the result of impending judgment.

Since the Egyptians believed in the universal sinfulness of humanity, it seems that no Egyptian had a chance for salvation. This was a tremendous theological dilemma. However, the Egyptians also believed that the heart could be stopped from naturally confessing sin so that salvation could still be possible. This was thought to be accomplished by placing a stone scarab beetle, shaped in the form of a heart, either in the mummified clothes encasing the deceased or tied to the chest. The scarab beetle was a symbol of the sun god, of whom Pharaoh was viewed as the incarnation, and they thought it had magical powers to suppress the heart's tendency to confess sin so that salvation could be secured. Thus it was actually the magical power of the divine Pharaoh that imposed this silence upon the heart and was responsible for the individual's salvation.

There were various magical spells written on the stone scarab heart to bring about the silence of the human heart. The magical power of the sun god (and Pharaoh) was believed to transfer the stillness of the stone heart to the deceased so that the heart's movements to confess sin would be transformed into the stonelike stillness of silence. This suppression of the heart's confession apparently came to be seen as a kind of "hardening of the heart."[5]

Could this immoral Egyptian concept of salvation through "hardening of the heart" be the background against which to understand the

---

5. For an argument supporting this contention see A. Hermann, "Das Steinhartes Herz," in *Jahrbuch für Antike und Christentum* 4 (Münster: Aschendorff'sche, 1961), 102–5. I have also argued this in my "The Exodus Hardening Motif of Yahweh as a Polemic," ThM Thesis, Dallas Theological Seminary (1976), 48–52.

Lord's hardening of Pharaoh's heart? Moses repeatedly commanded Pharaoh to let the people go, but God repeatedly hardened Pharaoh's heart so that he would not release Israel. But perhaps this was not the only purpose of the hardening of Pharaoh's heart. Whereas the pharaoh's magical hardening caused a nonconfession of sin and an apparent sinless heart, resulting in salvation, the Lord's hardening of Pharaoh's heart appears to have led to his own heart confessing sin (cf. Ex. 9:27, 34; 10:16–17) and acknowledging his sinfully heavy condition, resulting in judgment (cf. Ex. 14:4, 17–28). Whereas Pharaoh's hardening the hearts of others falsely suppressed sin, the Lord's hardening of Pharaoh's heart rightly revealed the monarch's sin.

The Lord's hardening of Pharaoh's heart may have been intended, in part, to show that the Egyptian way of salvation is a sham and was really the very opposite—a way of damnation. In fact, is it not interesting that the dead Pharaoh was the only Egyptian who did not have to go through the judgment process, but now, more than any other Egyptian in the exodus narrative, he is the focus of God's hardening judgment? It is probably no coincidentce that one of the Hebrew words used for the Lord's hardening of Pharaoh means "to make heavy." Ironically, the pharaoh who claimed to remove the sinful heaviness of others' hearts could not remove his own. The pharaoh himself had now "been weighed on the scales and found deficient" (Dan. 5:27) and awaited impending judgment at the Red Sea. Pharaoh's heart became literally like the stone heart that symbolized his power and ironically caused him to be hard and insensitive to God's commands, which led to his destruction. Because of his stone heart, he sank like a stone in the Red Sea.

Daniel's Accusers Snared by Their Own Trap

In the book of Daniel, there is a narrative account that begins with the mention of Daniel being promoted by the king to the office of "vice president" over all Persia. As a result, the other officials in the royal court became jealous and tried to find evidence of some misconduct, which would be grounds for accusation against Daniel. By so doing, they hoped the king would dismiss Daniel from his office. However, no wrongdoing could be found in him.

Therefore, they devised a plan that would ensure that Daniel would break the law. They persuaded King Darius to establish a temporary law whereby anyone who made a petition or prayer to any god or man besides the king for thirty days "shall be cast into the lions' den" (Dan. 6:7). No doubt, this flattered the king, but it also meant that Daniel would have to break the statute since he always prayed faithfully to his Lord three times a day.

Soon after the law was enacted, the enemies of Daniel brought evidence before the king that Daniel had violated the royal decree and had to suffer the penalty of capital punishment. The king was distressed because he loved Daniel, and he tried to figure out how he could deliver him. However, the king was forced to enact the penalty, since no law established by a Persian king could ever be revoked (Dan. 6:12–18). Although the king begrudgingly had Daniel thrown into the lions' den, he hoped that Daniel's God would deliver him.

The next morning the king's hopes were fulfilled, for God had delivered Daniel from the lions' mouths. Because of the injustice done to Daniel, the king ordered that Daniel's accusers be thrown into the lions' den. Daniel's fate recalls David's cry for divine vengeance upon Saul:

My soul is among lions;
I must lie among those who breathe forth fire,
Even the sons of men, whose teeth are spears and arrows,
And their tongue a sharp sword. . . .
My soul is bowed down;

> They dug a pit before me;
> They themselves have fallen into the midst of it. (Ps. 57:4, 6)

Perhaps the irony of this punishment is expressed in Daniel 6:24: "those men who had eaten the pieces [an Aramaic idiom translated as 'maliciously accused'] of Daniel" were cast into the pit, "and they had not reached the bottom of the den before the lions . . . crushed all their bones" to pieces with their mouths!

Ironic Judgment as the Rule, Not the Exception

Is this kind of retributive affliction the exception rather than the rule? The answer, I believe, is negative. In fact, I have already mentioned that Psalms and Proverbs abundantly testify to this form of chastisement. The testimony of these two books is significant because they present most of the statements in the form of generalizations or principles.

The expressions of ironic justice in the Psalms are found in David's prayers about the wicked, which are clearly generalized references either to the fate of a multitude of evil people or to his own personal enemies whose descriptions seem to transcend David's own situation.[6] So in Psalm 9:15, David speaks broadly of the nations of the earth who "have sunk down in the pit which they have made" and been caught "in the net which they hid" (see also Ps. 115:2–8). Likewise David speaks sweepingly of the wicked in Psalm 37:14–15 who "have drawn the sword" yet "their sword will enter their own heart." The universal tenor of the psalm is introduced in the first verse: "Do not fret because of evildoers; be not envious toward wrongdoers."

Proverbs especially emphasizes the universality of retributive irony by virtue of the kind of literature it is. Any particular proverb in the book arose from and is based on a wise person's, most

---

6. Many throughout church history have believed most of the psalms to have three references: (1) the individual psalmist (often David), (2) Christ, and (3) the corporate church. Augustine was one of the earliest church commentators to hold this view.

especially Solomon's, long experience of observing life. A prover-
bial saying develops through a lifetime of observing various events
and comparing them. In fact, the Hebrew word for *proverb* literally
means "comparison" or "likeness." As the wise man compares all
these various events, he begins to see that some are similar, and this
reveals a universal principle in some pithy saying. For instance, the
proverb "like mother, like daughter" (e.g., Ezek. 16:44) arose originally from observing homes in which children had a tendency to
be like their parents. So a general principle was discerned, that the
mother's relation to her daughter influences to a significant degree
the daughter's personality or character. Similarly, the saying "Haste
makes waste" is a broad principle derived from frequently observing
that a task finished too quickly results in failure (similarly, "The early
bird catches the worm").

Accordingly, the maxims of ironic punishment in Proverbs are
also expressions of a general principle inherent in the warp and woof
of moral reality. Proverbs 28:10 reads, "He who leads the upright
astray in an evil way will himself fall into his own pit." The author
had observed that those who tried to mislead the godly into some
misfortune ended up misleading themselves to their own collapse.
Probably one of the most significant proverbs for punitive irony is
Proverbs 16:25, which has already been mentioned: "There is a way
which seems right to a man, but its end is the way of death." No doubt
Solomon repeatedly observed that what at first seemed to be the best
course of action turned out to be the worst. His own actions ended
up condemning him. Consequently, ironic justice, far from being an
exceptional phenomenon, is a pattern of life.

Ironic Judgment of Individuals and Nations

That this sort of irony is the rule rather than the exception in the Old
Testament is also borne out by numerous other examples where it is

observed in biblical history. When Nadab and Abihu, Aaron's sons, sinned by offering "strange fire" (burnt offerings) to the Lord, they were punished by fire coming out from the presence of the Lord, which killed them (Lev. 10:1–2).[7] Israel ungratefully murmured against the Lord in the wilderness when they grew tired of the manna and "greedily desired" the meat they used to eat in Egypt (Num. 11:4–23). Therefore, God vented his wrath by giving them so much meat that it spoiled and killed those who had been so greedy. In fact, their graves were called "the graves of craving" (v. 35), for ironically "the greedy found their graves while giving vent to their greedy desires."[8]

When Naboth refused to sell his vineyard to the spoiled and greedy King Ahab, Jezebel incited her husband Ahab to have Naboth falsely accused of publicly cursing God, the penalty of which would be death by stoning. And so two men were bribed to bring false charges against innocent Naboth, and he was stoned. Immediately thereafter God pronounced the punishment that would eventually come upon Ahab for his dastardly deed: "In the place where the dogs licked up the blood of Naboth the dogs will lick up your blood" (1 Kings 21:19). Soon thereafter Ahab died in battle, "and the dogs licked up his blood . . . according to the word of the LORD which He spoke" (1 Kings 22:38). The same fate also later befell Jezebel (2 Kings 9:26, 33–37).

The evil king of the Canaanites, Adoni-bezek, was defeated by Israel, and they "cut off his thumbs and big toes" because he had unjustly "cut off" the "thumbs and big toes" of seventy other kings. He then confessed, "As I have done, so God has repaid me" (Judg. 1:6–7). Likewise, because Abimelech wrongly killed "seventy men, on one stone" (Judg. 9:5), "a certain woman threw an upper millstone on Abi-

---

7. See Pink, *Life of David*, 66, who has observed this irony.
8. See A. P. Ross, "Popular Etymology and Paranomasia in the Old Testament," PhD diss., University of Cambridge (1982), 210, who explains the ironic significance of this incident.

melech's head, crushing his skull" (Judg. 9:53). "Thus God repaid the wickedness of Abimelech" (Judg. 9:56; cf. v. 57). The priest Eli wrongly "honored" (literally "made heavy") his sinful sons and so God punished him by making the sons "lightly esteemed" (literally "light") before his sight (cf. 1 Sam. 2:29–30). Their "despising" of God led to God's "contempt" of them. Just as Joab murdered righteous men, so it was pronounced, "The Lord will return his blood on his own head" and he was "put . . . to death, and he was buried" (1 Kings 2:32, 34).

Throughout the Old Testament ironic judgments are executed especially upon wicked nations. Babylon had been particularly brutal in destroying Israel, even to the extent of killing infants. Therefore, the psalmist issues the following imprecation upon them:

> How blessed will be the one who repays you
> With the recompense with which you have repaid us.
> How blessed will be the one who seizes and dashes your
>   little ones
> Against the rock. (Ps. 137:8–9)

Because Babylon had devoured, plundered, preyed upon, looted, and made Israel naked, so they were to be chastised by suffering the exact same fate at the hands of other nations (see Jer. 30:16; Hab. 2:8; 2:15–16).[9] Latter-day Babylon will likewise be judged (Rev. 18:5–7). As the nations surrounding Israel had defeated them and "sold the sons of Judah and Jerusalem to the Greeks . . . also I [God] will sell your sons and your daughters (of the surrounding nations) into the hands of Judah, and they will sell them . . . to a distant nation" (Joel 3:6–8).[10]

---

9. These references were brought to my attention by P. D. Miller in his paper, "A Classification of the Patterns of Correspondence [in Judicial Punishment]," read at the Old Testament Seminar at the University of Cambridge (1978).

10. Miller, "A Classification of the Patterns of Correspondence [in Judicial Punishment]."

Of course, Israel was not exempt from such judgments. When they "rejected the law of the LORD" (Amos 2:4), God judged them by sending "a famine on the land," so that the Israelites would "go to and fro to seek the word of the LORD, but . . . not find it" (Amos 8:11–12). God judged their sin of rejecting his word by removing it from Israel so that his word could no longer be found. In practice, this meant that God would send no more prophets to Israel for a period.

Has not the same tragic irony happened to a significant degree in the Israel of God today, the church of the twenty-first century? The church together with many of the theological seminaries have rejected the authority and relevance of God's word so that today it is relatively rare to hear the Bible preached in many churches. It is as if God has said, "If you want to reject the authority of my word in Scripture, I will spurn you by no longer speaking to you in any way." This is understandable since God has designed his revelation during the church age normatively to come through Scripture. But there are many in churches today who long to hear a word from God but do not. I pray that the church's rejection of God's word is not so complete that he completely rejects communicating through it. The church is being ironically punished by its own sin: the more it rejects God's word, the more God rejects it.

The principle by which God judged all nations in the Old Testament is summarized in Obadiah 15:

> For the day of the LORD draws near on all the nations.
> As you have done, it will be done to you.
> Your dealings will return on your own head.

So also Isaiah's pronouncement of judgment on Assyria would appear generally applicable to other nations:

Woe to you, O destroyer. . . .
As soon as you finish destroying, you shall be destroyed;
As soon as you cease to deal treacherously, others will deal
    treacherously with you. (Isa. 33:1)[11]

Proverbs 1 also states the principle on an individual level, but, as we have seen, it is likewise relevant for nations:

My son, if sinners entice you,
Do not consent.
If they say, "Come with us,
Let us lie in wait for blood,
Let us ambush the innocent . . ."
They lie in wait for their own blood;
They ambush their own lives.
So are the ways of everyone who gains by violence;
It takes away the life of its possessors. (1:10–11, 18–19)

However, even in the face of such evidence, many may still insist that God's ironic judgment of the ungodly is uncommon. The primary reason for this insistence lies in the observation that in both ancient and modern times those who live wicked lives usually get away with it. It appears that the godless never get their just deserts in this life. How many people in the business world cheat their way to financial success, live long, luxurious lives, and die wealthy in their old age?

Solomon observed the same phenomenon: "I have seen everything during my lifetime of futility; there is a righteous man who perishes in his righteousness and there is a wicked man who prolongs his life in his wickedness" (Eccles. 7:15; cf. 8:14). However, Solomon also asserted from an eternal perspective that

---

11. With respect to the references to Jeremiah, Obadiah, and Isaiah, see Miller, "A Classification of the Patterns of Correspondence [in Judicial Punishment]."

although a sinner does evil a hundred times and may lengthen his life, . . . [it] will not be well for the evil man and he will not lengthen his days like a shadow [everlastingly], because he does not fear [believe in] God. (Eccles. 8:12–13; see also 12:13–14)

Walter Kaiser says of these two passages, "The wicked may appear to be getting away with murder . . . but such sinning with seeming impunity will finally be judged by the living God"[12] (see also Ps. 73:1–20). The final judgment by God involves the ultimate irony of unbelief, in which all the evil a man has gotten away with in this life will be poured back on his head in the afterlife.

Yet even before the final judgment, it can be said that all unbelievers begin to be punished in this life, although they may experience worldly success. This punishment is of a spiritual or invisible nature: "For the wrath of God is revealed from heaven against all ungodliness and unrighteousness of men, who suppress the truth in unrighteousness" (Rom. 1:18). And "he who believes in the Son has eternal life; but he who does not obey the Son will not see life, but the wrath of God abides on him" even now (John 3:36; cf. 3:18). Not to believe in Christ is to be separated from God, which is a punishment in itself and will be extended into eternity if unbelief persists until physical death. In this sense, there really are no exceptions to the ironic punishment of unbelievers in their earthly lives. Their ultimate trust in some aspect of this world is the very thing causing their present spiritual failure and judgment. That this is the case is well illustrated in the history of Israel.

Little Boy Blue

Non-Christians can break the force of God's ironic judgment only by trusting in Christ as their savior, the one who took their judgment

---

12. Walter C. Kaiser Jr., *Ecclesiastes, Total Life*, Everyman's Bible Commentary (Chicago: Moody, 1979), 91.

upon himself at the cross. We will speak more of this in the following pages.

I hope that no Christian is reading this and thinking that he or she is exempt from God's ironic forms of judgment. Although Christians will not suffer eternal judgment, they are not exempt from other temporal kinds of punishment. Christians can commit sins in the business world, family, church, and social relationships. If this sin is not confessed to the Lord with a repentant heart, the Lord may use such sin as the very thing that disciplines the sinner.

The song "Cats in the Cradle and the Silver Spoon" by Harry Chapin captures one aspect of the subtlety of this danger for Christian and non-Christian alike. The famous song is about a father who was not home much while his son was growing up. The father was gone so much that he did not get to see his son learn to walk or to throw a ball. As the years pass, the young son expresses his desire to be just like his father one day. Eventually he goes off to college, and when he returns home on school break, the father wants to sit down and catch up with his son, but the son is more interested in borrowing his father's car. The father begins to realize that his son got his wish—he's grown up to be just like his father. Eventually, after the son has moved away and developed his own life, his father calls and inquires about a visit. But the son is too busy with his job and his family, and as he says goodbye, he adds, "It's sure nice talking to you, Dad." When the father hangs up the telephone, he realized with sad irony just how like him his son has become.[13]

There are many ways that we as Christians can be caught in an ironic web of subtle sin. How can we increasingly break out of this web? Of course, the only way to begin to break out of this matrix of sin is to trust in the irony of salvation—that the perfectly righteous

---

13. The lyrics of the song can be found at https://www.songfacts.com/lyrics/harry-chapin/cats-in-the-cradle.

Jesus experienced the judgment that sinners deserve and that we, who are guilty of sin, are declared righteous because of Christ's work at the cross, which is imputed to us. For those who have believed, I offer three encouragements to help them be able to progress in coming out of sins in which they are entangled (cf. Heb. 12:1).

First, read and study God's word daily so that you may be more sensitive to subtle but dangerous sin and how to overcome it. John says in his first epistle that Christians can become strong through allowing the word of God to abide in them, which will result in "overcoming the evil one" (1 John 2:14). When we do not read God's word, we do not know what God expects of us, and we are more likely to sin.

This first suggestion may appear elementary but, in reality, it is profound and important. It is like the relationship I have with my wife. She does most of the shopping for the family. When we first got married she would buy things I didn't like, and sometimes, even when she bought things I did like, she spent what I thought was too much money. However, now that we have been married for some years, we have come to know each other much more intimately. We are more familiar with each other's tastes and desires. Now when my wife shops, she has a better idea of my tastes and financial desires. In fact, she even occasionally trusts me to shop for the household, since I also have become better acquainted with her personal penchants.

It is the same with the Lord. The more we read his word, the more familiar we become with his mind and character, and the more we are apt to respond the way he would, even in "gray" situations that Scripture does not explicitly address (e.g., whom to marry, what job to take, etc.). Paul says as much in Romans 12:2: "Do not be conformed to this world, but be transformed by the renewing of your mind [in Scripture], so that you may prove what the will of God is, that which is good and acceptable and perfect." The more transformed to Christ's image we become (Rom. 8:29), the more we will respond to life's choices in the way Christ would. And we will be able increasingly to avoid the ironic pitfalls that otherwise could occur.

In addition to a daily reading of Scripture, a second suggestion is being willing to apply God's word to our life by faith. It is not enough to know God's word—we must be willing, by faith, to allow it to mold our lives.

Finally, we should come to God in prayer daily, confessing our sin with a repentant attitude.

When we refuse to follow these three basic biblical injunctions, we become rebellious, like David, and God often breaks down such rebellion by putting into motion his ironic justice.

These recommendations, which are really biblical commands, might seem simplistic to some Christians, but Christians are never too mature not to heed them. Indeed, the book of Proverbs repeatedly calls people "simple" and "naive" who don't continually pay heed to these recommendations. After getting married, my wife and I were preparing to leave our home in the United States to undertake theological study overseas. After the last worship service at our home church, an elderly Christian man gave some spiritual advice about my marriage. He told me, "You two seek the Lord through the word and prayer, and you won't have to worry about major problems in your relationship with each other." I recall thinking that while I appreciated the intent of his advice, it seemed elementary and therefore superficial. However, it is the best and truest advice that I have ever received. It is astonishingly difficult to stay consistently in God's word and prayer, especially as a couple, and it takes discipline to do so. Couples who don't so seek the Lord may think their relationship is good, but ironically it becomes spiritually worse the longer they neglect him. My wife and I have observed that the welfare of our relationship is directly dependent on the degree to which we seek God through his word and prayer. We have noticed that when we neglect this, we are also neglecting the health of our relationship.

A Reflection on Ironic Judgment

My comments in the preceding section are most relevant for those who have trusted in Christ rather than themselves for their destiny. But what implications does the biblical idea of ironic judgment have for those who have not so committed their life? Scripture says, "Who has believed our message? . . . All of us like sheep have gone astray, each of us has turned to his own way" (Isa. 53:1, 6). We have walked in a way that is not good, following our own thoughts (Isa. 65:2), and as people "have chosen their own ways . . . so I [God] will choose their punishments" (Isa. 66:3–4). The Lord has "set before you the way of life and the way of death" (Jer. 21:8). "Now therefore, thus says the LORD of hosts, 'Consider your ways!'" (Hag. 1:5). "Let the wicked forsake His way. . . . 'For My thoughts are not your thoughts, nor are your ways My ways'" (Isa. 55:7–8).

Consider that God has "made known . . . the ways of life" (Acts 2:28). For Jesus Christ is "the way, and the truth, and the life; no one comes to the Father but through" him (John 14:6). Although "each of us has turned to his own way, . . . the LORD has caused the iniquity of us all to fall on Him. . . . He was cut off out of the land of the living for the transgression of [God's] people to whom the stroke was due. . . . And He Himself bore the sin of many" on the cross (Isa. 53:6, 8, 12). Therefore, commit your way to the Lord Jesus Christ and do not forsake the Way (Acts 9:2), for Christ is the only one who is able to "guide our feet into the way of peace" (Luke 1:79).

In an age when many theologians believe that God's love means he could never ultimately send anyone to eternal hell, Jesus's words in Matthew 7 have never been more relevant:

Enter through the narrow gate; for the gate is wide and the way is broad that leads to destruction, and there are many who enter through it. For the gate is small and the way is narrow that leads to life, and there are few who find it. (vv. 13–14)

Learning from the Parable of the Frog

What so often seems to be the right way is the wrong way from God's viewpoint. The way that people think will lead to success and blessing really often leads to the opposite, failure and cursing. And frequently the sinful way that a person thinks will ensure that prosperity is the very way that secures the person's adversity. In other words, people are punished by the very means in which they attempt to get ahead (so Pharaoh, Haman, Saul, and Judas). And it is God who sees to it that a person's sinful ways to obtain good welfare are reversed, so that it becomes a one-way street at whose end is only affliction. God is always at work turning the apparent blessing of the wicked into actual cursing.

A person's ironic plight in life is too often like that of the unaware and contented frog, as narrated some years ago by the family counselor James Dobson:

> Nature has generously equipped most animals with a fear of things that could be harmful to them. Their survival depends on recognition of a particular danger in time to avoid it. But good old mother nature did not protect the frog quite so well; she overlooked a serious flaw in his early warning system that sometimes proves fatal. If a frog is placed in a pan of warm water under which the heat is being increased very gradually, he will typically show no inclination to escape. Since he is a cold-blooded creature, his body temperature remains approximately the same as the water around him and he does

not notice the slow change taking place. As the temperature continues to intensify, the frog remains oblivious to his danger; he could easily hop his way to safety, but he is apparently thinking about something else. He will just sit there, contentedly peering over the edge of the pan while the steam curls ominously around his nostrils. Eventually the boiling frog will pass on to his reward, having succumbed to an unnecessary misfortune that he could easily have avoided.[14]

Like the frog, people are often content with their unbelieving ways, unaware that they will lead to destruction. Mankind also has a crucial flaw in his warning system against sin that can be fatal. All people are born under the influence of Adam's "original sin," which spiritually blinds them to the impending danger of their persistent sinful ways. As the frog, they have no inclination of "fleeing from the wrath to come" (Matt. 3:7). People could escape into the arms of Christ, but they apparently think their own way is at least as good.

If you haven't trusted in Christ, do not wait to flee into his arms from your burning plight, lest it become too late. Just as the steam begins to rise over the unsuspecting frog, so already upon the unbeliever "the wrath of God abides on him" (John 3:36), and presently "the wrath of God is revealed from heaven against" him (Rom. 1:18). Such earthly wrath is but the simmering prelude to "their fire [that] shall not be quenched" (Isa. 66:24) and to "the smoke of their torment," which will go up forever and ever (Rev. 14:11). Being hard-hearted and insensitive to their perilous situation, they think they are on the road to happiness, when, on the contrary, they are headed only for despair. Is there an irony being played out in your life that may lead to destruction?

Truly, "there is a way which seems right to a man, but its end is the way of death" (Prov. 14:12).

---

14. James Dobson, *Dare to Discipline* (New York: Bantam, 1982), 5.

2

People Resemble the
Idols They Worship

We know that there is no such thing as an idol in the world,
and that there is no God but one.

—The apostle Paul (1 Cor. 8:4)

Contemporary America might well be called the "imitation generation." A variety of images are continually set before us through
a number of mediums, and we often copy them. Television com-
mercials are based on the hope that viewers will conform their
lives to the suggested images being advertised. At the height of
its popularity in the 1980s the television series *Dallas* inspired a
Western-style clothing fad from California to New York. Indeed,
there is serious concern among television critics that Americans
are conforming their lives to too many of the media images. For
example, some see a correlation between shows depicting sexual

scenes and violence to an actual increase of immorality and crime in society.

A friend of mine who often travels observed that before 1950 he could tour through the United States and discern peculiar characteristics of different parts of the country. Now he does not notice as much diversity and wonders whether the increasing conformity of clothing, language, architecture, and recreation is due to the media's influence.

In the 1960s, many young people imitated the Beatles' hairstyles, and even today some still try to reflect the figure of Elvis Presley. No doubt, all of us have imitated to some degree a particular peer group.

This human trait to reflect surrounding images is well illustrated in children. When our son, Stephen, was a little over two years old, we began to notice how much he was imitating my wife and me. He played hide-and-seek with his animals like we played with him. He read stories to his animals; he gave them medicine and spanked them. He talked on his toy phone the way we did (even with a Texas accent!) and he played like he was giving his toy animals medicine in the same way their mother cooked on the stove. When our two daughters were born, they followed the same pattern. They cooked on their toy stove in the same way their mother cooked on her stove.

Why do human beings have this intrinsic tendency to reflect images around them? Genesis 1 and 2 supply the reason. God made man and woman to be creatures who imitate. Originally, they were created to reflect the image of their Creator. However, when they sinned, they decided not to conform their life to God's image but to the image of the serpent's sinful and deceptive character. Ever since, the human tendency has been to reflect part of the creation rather than the Creator.

Consequently, a person's character is never "in neutral"—it was not created to be. One is being conformed either to some earthly image or to God's image. Romans 12:2 says that either you are being conformed to the world or you are being transformed into the image of God by the renewing of your mind in his word. What happens to us when we don't reflect God's image? Or, to put it another way, what does it mean to become conformed to the world? The background for this New Testament idea is to be found in the Old Testament concept of idol worship.[1]

The Irony of Idolatry: Becoming Like What We Worship (Isaiah 6:9–13)

Children begin what we continue to do as adults. We imitate. We reflect. Sometimes consciously, sometimes unconsciously. Do you remember being part of a peer group? Perhaps you can think back to a group from middle school, high school, or college, and to one degree or another, whether consciously or unconsciously, how you reflected and resembled that peer group. Maybe many of you wore shirts with an alligator logo, and you did not feel a part of the group unless your shirt had an alligator on it. Maybe you desired to belong to an athletic group, and to be accepted in the group you pursued athletics. Hopefully, you were not in peer groups that, as there are many today and have been in past years, one needs to participate in drugs or some other destructive activity to be accepted. Though we may not want to admit it, all of us as humans sometimes reflect what we are around, often subtly and unconsciously. Often we reflect things in our culture and our society. In Isaiah 6:9–13, we see what Israel reflected in their culture:

---

1. The rest of this chapter is based on a sermon delivered in the Chapel of Gordon-Conwell Theological Seminary in the spring of 1987, which had its origin in 1983 in a brief section of a rough-draft book on biblical irony, which was never published. This sermon was expanded into an article: G. K. Beale, "Isaiah VI 9–13: A Retributive Taunt Against Idolatry," *Vetus Testamentum* 41 (1991): 257–78. This article was expanded into a lengthy chapter in G. K. Beale, *We Become What We Worship* (Downers Grove: InterVarsity, 2008), 36–70.

He [God] said, "Go, and tell this people:

> 'Keep on listening, but do not perceive;
> Keep on looking, but do not understand.'
> Render the hearts of this people insensitive,
> Their ears dull,
> And their eyes dim,
> Otherwise they might see with their eyes,
> Hear with their ears,
> Understand with their hearts,
> And return and be healed."

Then I said, "Lord, how long?" And He answered,

> "Until cities are devastated and without inhabitant,
> Houses are without people,
> And the land is utterly desolate,
> "The LORD has removed men far away,
> And the forsaken places are many in the midst of the
> land.
> Yet there will be a tenth portion in it,
> And it will again be subject to burning,
> Like a terebinth or an oak
> Whose stump remains when it is felled.
> The holy seed is its stump."

What does this passage say that Israel predominantly reflected? We can see it on both a conscious and an unconscious level. And as we see what they reflected, let us ask ourselves if there is anything in our culture today that we reflect. We can also see in this passage what Israel should have reflected. I would like to ask you what you predominantly reflect in your life. As you look at yourself, how would you ultimately describe what you reflect? What do you resemble from the world around you?

Verses 9-10 are a command to Isaiah to make the people blind through his preaching. Commentators have been so dumbfounded by this that one has even said that Isaiah really didn't have this vision, but at the end of his ministry, having failed as a preacher and counselor, he decided to blame his failure on God. According to this view, God absolves Isaiah because the hardening was his plan all along, so Isaiah realizes that he truly succeeded. But that particular view doesn't represent a high view of Scripture, and I don't think a careful interpretation of Isaiah 6 could support such a view.

So what are we to make of this difficult language? If God appeared to you (and I pray he will not appear to you in this way) and said, "When you go teach my word, I want you to harden peoples' hearts so they won't be saved, so they will go out and be destroyed," I am sure you would seek counsel, or you might keep reading the Scriptures and look for another word from the Lord. Isaiah did not though. What is going on here? How in the world can we make sense of this passage and still believe in a good God who cares for his flock?

It is important to get a wider perspective on the context of verses 9-13. Isaiah 6 has four parts: verses 1-4; verses 5-7; verses 8-10; and verses 11-13. In verses 1-4, God is praised for his holiness:

Holy, Holy, Holy is the LORD of Hosts,
The whole earth is full of His glory. (v. 3)

Because God is set apart in his attributes in a way that no one else is, he is perfect in every attribute, not only in moral purity. So he is to be glorified for all his attributes. He is to be respected for his weighty attributes. The Hebrew word for *glory* sometimes means "weighty."

After we find that God is glorified for his holiness, God chooses someone to represent the very tiny, pure remnant of Israel who is not holy. And it is Isaiah. In verses 5–7, we find that Isaiah, even though sinful, is declared to be holy by the forgiving grace of God. Isaiah says in verse 5:

> I am a man of unclean lips,
> And I live among a people of unclean lips;
> For my eyes have seen the King, the LORD of hosts."

In verse 6, a seraph comes to Isaiah with burning coals in his hand. In verse 7 he touches Isaiah's mouth to symbolize that Isaiah has experienced the forgiving grace of God. Isaiah is declared holy by the God who is holy, and Isaiah's life is to be lived to the redounding of the glory of God. He hasn't made himself holy; God has declared him to be holy. Therefore, Isaiah is one who reveres God and resembles him, resulting in restoration (Isa. 6:5–7).

What You Revere, You Resemble, Either for Ruin or Restoration, Part 1 (Isaiah 6:8–10)

Isaiah reveres God, but there is a problem. After witnessing God's holiness glorified (vv. 1–4) and Isaiah's life declared holy even though sinful (vv. 5–7), we find in verses 8–10 the verdict pronounced on Israel:

> I heard the voice of the Lord saying, "Whom shall I send, and who will go for Us?" Then [Isaiah] said, "Here I am. Send me!" [God] said, "Go and tell this people:
>
>> 'Keep on listening, but do not perceive;
>> Keep on looking, but do not understand.'
>> "Render the hearts of this people insensitive,
>> Their ears dull,

And their eyes dim,
Otherwise they might see with their eyes,
Hear with their ears,
Understand with their hearts,
And return and be healed."

What are we to make of this? It is certainly a verdict of guilty for Israel. But why such a harsh verdict? Is this a cruel lightning bolt sent by God out of the Isaianic blue? How can God be good and just, if that is the case? We find that there is a reason for Isaiah's ministry. The timing of Isaiah's call comes after many hundreds of years during which Israel has unrepentantly sinned, and now a declaration of guilty is coming upon this generation. So this is not a lightning bolt out of the blue. As we look at the context of Isaiah in depth, it makes sense of these words, and it makes sense of the justice of God. Israel is being judged because of unrepentant sins.

Whenever the prophets use what we might call sensory organ–malfunction language—whenever people's organs are depicted as not functioning—without exception, it refers not just to sinners in general but to sinners who are idolaters.

Isaiah elsewhere sees that idolaters are people who have ears but can't hear and eyes but can't see. He says that those who trust in idols will be put to shame (42:17), as will those who say to molten images, "You are gods." God addresses these idol worshipers:

Hear, you deaf!
And look, you blind, that you may see.
Who is blind but My servant,
Or so deaf as My messenger whom I send?
Who is so blind as he that is at peace with Me,
Or so blind as the servant of the LORD?

> You have seen many things, but you do not observe them;
>
> Your ears are open, but none hears. (42:18–20)

This is repeated throughout Isaiah, and in this respect, Isaiah 44:17–18 is similar:

> But the rest of [the tree] he makes into a god, his graven image. He falls down before it and worships; he also prays to it and says, "Deliver me, for you are my god."

God is speaking here not just about the Gentile idol worshipers, but about Israel. Those who cut trees down and make part of them into idols should be addressed the way we see in verse 18: "They do not know, nor do they understand, for He [God] has smeared over their eyes so they cannot see and their hearts so they cannot comprehend." Here, idol worshipers are said to be those who do not have eyes, even though they have physical eyes. And even though they have physical ears, they do not hear spiritually.

In Isaiah 6, the people are said to have eyes that do not see and ears that do not hear. I think the reason is that they are idol worshipers. The reason idolaters are described as people whose sensory organs malfunction is found in Isaiah, but I want to look first at Psalm 115 (see also Ps. 135:15–18), where we see the reason spelled out clearly. Psalm 115 speaks of the idols of the pagans:

> Their idols are silver and gold,
>
> The work of man's hands.
>
> They have mouths but they cannot speak,
>
> They have eyes but they cannot see,
>
> They have ears but they cannot hear. . . .
>
> Those who make them will become like them,
>
> Everyone who trusts in them. (vv. 4, 8)

The principle is this: if you worship idols, you will become like the idols, and that likeness will ruin you. If you read Isaiah 1–5, you'll see that one of Israel's main sins, not coincidentally, was idol worship:

> Their land has also been filled with idols,
> They worship the work of their hands
> That which their fingers made. (Isa. 2:8)

> But the idols will completely vanish.
> Men will go into caves of the rocks
> And into holes of the ground
> Before the terror of the LORD. . . .
> In that day men will cast away to the moles and the bats
> Their idols of silver and their idols of gold,
> Which they made for themselves to worship. (vv. 18–20)

Israel's problem was idol worship. Isaiah 6:9 can be paraphrased in the following way: "Isaiah, go and tell this idolatrous people that they have been so unrepentant about their idol worship that I am going to make them as spiritually insensitive as the idols, as spiritually inanimate as the idols. You like idols, Israel? All right, you are going to become like an idol, and that is the judgment." It is the old *lex talionis*—an eye for an eye—of the Old Testament. People are punished by means of their own sin, and this is a paramount example of it. It is just as in eternity when God says, "You didn't want to spend your life in fellowship with me and my people on this earth. All right, I will give you what you wanted on this earth for eternity—separation from God."

Here in Isaiah 6:9–10, Israel is being given what they want, from a certain perspective. They are ironically punished by means of their own sin. The idols have physical eyes and ears, but they could not actually see or hear. Even more, the idols could not spiritually hear or see, though a god was supposed to underlie all idols. Israel is commanded to become like the idols, and that is their judgment. In verses 8–10, God is pronouncing through Isaiah that Israel will be judged by being made spiritually insensitive like the idols they worship. Israel will become as blind and deaf spiritually as the spiritually blind and deaf idols. If you look up "ears" and "eyes" in a concordance, you will find that wherever Israel is reprimanded for idol worship, they are often addressed as those who have eyes but cannot see and ears but cannot hear.

Isaiah 6:9–10 is an allusion to Deuteronomy 29:4, which says to the first generation of Israel, "To this day I am not giving you eyes to see or ears to hear or a heart to understand." That first generation was characterized by idolatry, as 1 Corinthians 10 says. And Deuteronomy 4:28 even says that the idols have eyes and ears and other traits, but they really can't perceive. So even the first generation of Israelites was idolatrous, and the generation in Isaiah's time is just like that first generation.

It is no coincidence that after Israel worships the golden calf at the foot of Mount Sinai (Ex. 32), God judges them by not giving them "a heart to know, nor eyes to see, nor ears to hear" (Deut. 29:4). Israel had become as spiritually inanimate as the golden calf idol that they were worshiping, which is clear from the narrative in Exodus 32. Just as cattle are hard to steer because they are "stiff-necked," break their yokes, go out of control, veer from the desired way, and need to be regathered and led again, so similarly did Israel. As a result of worshiping the calf idol, Israel is said to be "stiff-necked" (Ex. 32:9; 33:3, 5; 34:9), "unbound" (or "let loose," 32:25), as having "quickly turned aside from the way which [God] commanded them" (32:8), and as needing to be "gathered together" (32:26) and led again (32:34). They had become just as spiritually rebellious as the cattle that were symbolized by their idol, which they worshiped (see also Deut. 9:12–16).

This cattle-like rebellion of idol worship influenced later generations of Israelites who repeated the abomination. Indeed, like father, like son. In Deuteronomy 31 Moses predicts that future generations of Israelites will also worship idols (31:18; cf. 32:16–17) and become "stiff-necked" (31:27) and "turn from the way" (31:29). Indeed, Moses's prophecy was fulfilled repeatedly. During the reign of King Ahaz, Israel "stiffened their neck" and "made for themselves molten images, even two calves" (2 Kings 17:14–16). Nehemiah says of the later Israelite descendants, "They turned a stubborn shoulder and stiffened their neck. . . . However, You bore with them for many years, . . . yet they would not give ear" (Neh. 9:29–31). Hosea remarks that because of idol worship (Hos. 3:4; 4:12, 13, 17), "Israel is stubborn like a stubborn heifer; can the LORD now pasture them . . . ? Ephraim is joined to idols. Let him alone" (Hos. 4:16–17).

So the first generation of Israel, later generations, and Isaiah's generation grew spiritually lifeless like the idols they worshiped. The principle for them and us is, what you revere, you resemble, either for ruin or restoration.

Application of the Idolatry Principle in Isaiah 6:8–10

In the case of Israel, what they revered, they resembled for their ruin. How does this relate to us today? How can we bridge the gap between Old Testament idol worship and our contemporary time? We don't fall down to idols. I would dare say that there is no one in our Western culture who does this, though possibly with the increase of witchcraft, that kind of idolatry could be occurring.

The first bridge is the New Testament. What is said in the New Testament about idol worship? Paul already sees that idol worship goes beyond simply falling down at some statue. In Ephesians 5 and Colossians 3 he says that covetousness and greed are idolatry. Paul spiritualizes idolatry. Money then, like today, was an idol. An idol is any substitute for God. The Oxford English Dictionary defines *religion* as "a thing that one is devoted to," which can be God or something else. In fact, 1 John concludes with a short verse: "Little children, guard yourselves from idols" (5:21). I had formerly thought that besides wrong doctrine about Christ having been introduced by the false teachers, John's readers also had the problem of idol worship. I no longer think that is right. That last little verse is to be interpreted contextually in light of the entire book. A false view of Christ, John is saying, is a substitute for the true Christ, and that is idol worship. John is saying, "Beware of the false teachers who are introducing false teaching about Christ, and if you are sucked in by them, you are an idol worshiper."

The fact that the Bible says that the earth must be destroyed at the end of time is, I think, related to idolatry. The ultimate idol must be destroyed, and there must be a new heavens and earth untainted by the sin of Adam and Eve and their progeny, who were ultimately idol worshipers. The ultimate thing in which people take security, some aspect of the world, must be destroyed.

Israel worshiped idols for the same reasons the Athenians did. The apostle Paul saw an altar dedicated to the idol of the unknown God in Athens (Acts 17:23). The Athenians wanted to be sure they did not leave out any god who could prosper them, in case there was a god they did not recognize. Israel worshiped the gods of the Canaanites. It was not that they were trying to reject the Lord, necessarily, but they chose to worship these other gods too to try to assure a double dip of prosperity. Israel worshiped gods of fertility so that their children, flocks, and crops would flourish.

I would dare say that many idols today are for economic prosperity. When people commit to money and material possessions more than to God, money becomes an idol, and then suddenly, at least symbolically, they begin to have their ultimate security in the excessive trappings of their money, jewels, beautiful clothes, cars, and houses; they place their trust in financial security, which is idolatry, and they literally begin to take on the appearance of the wealth in which they have trusted.

What you commit to, you become; what you revere, you resemble, either for ruin or for restoration. Proverbs 14:12 says, "There is a way which seems right to a man, but its end is the way of death." Israel thought the idols were going to lead to prosperity and success and happiness, but ironically they led to the opposite, to their ruin.

Some people have hobbies as their idol. What people fill their time with is sometimes a mark, an emblem, of what they worship. Sports are a great example. Sometimes a sport takes such dedication that it becomes the top priority over everything else in one's life. Another idol is the media, which can subtly conform us to the world rather than to Christ. A Christian sociologist has said:

> In contrast to the men and women of the scriptures, many Christians sense only weakly the way God intervenes in the world and in each individual life; most Christians find it difficult to develop a daily awareness of God as Sovereign Lord, who holds the initiative in his dealing with us every day. This difficulty of not being aware of the Lord is partly due, he says, to our immersion in the media view of the world, where there is absent awareness of God and his ability to work his will in every circumstance of life.[2]

I am sure that many of us watch television, often when we want to sit back like leeches and relax and not use our minds. I was alarmed when I discovered from a survey some years ago that the typical American family spent an average of five hours a day every year watching television. We in the West are absorbed with television, computers, iPhones, or other forms of media. It is a form of relaxation, but we can become uncritically open to the media worldview. Subtly, unconsciously, we filter this worldview into our minds. And what is this worldview? It is the

---

2. Kevin Perrotta, "Television's Mind-Boggling Danger," *Christianity Today*, May 7, 1983, 21.

worldview that has no awareness of or sensitivity to God's working in the details of our everyday life.

When was the last time you saw a television series deal with a dilemma in the storyline by saying, "Let us look at the Scriptures and see what God says about this and then pray about it"? Or when have you heard on such a show, "Let us go to Pastor So-and-So to see what Scripture says about this problem"? No, you have not heard that, and if you heard it, you would jump up and say, "Wow! Listen to this! This is unusual." Subtly but surely, such programs tell us that it is unnatural to think of the things of the Lord in the details of our life. The worldview is that God is not active. And it makes us feel a little bit abnormal in relating to God and being sensitive to his sovereign dealings in our daily life, and we feel awkward about mentioning this feeling to anyone. I would dare say that we have been more influenced by the media than we want to admit. We come to reflect the worldview of this idol, which can destroy us. The same can be true with an oversaturation of the Internet.

One friend of mine defines *worldliness* in the following way: "Worldliness is whatever any culture does to make sin seem normal and righteousness seem strange."[3] And that is what the worldly media does to us. When we become conformed to a particular sin that our culture considers normal, that sin becomes an idol to which we become committed. What are you committed to? What are you being conformed to? Are you becoming like something in the world or like God as you perceive him in his word?

What You Revere, You Resemble, Either for Ruin or Restoration, Part 2 (Isaiah 6:11–13)

So far, then, the idea of Isaiah 6:1–10 has been that what you revere, you resemble, either for ruin or restoration. We must return to

---

3. David Wells, *God in the Wasteland: The Reality of Truth in a World of Fading Dreams* (Grand Rapids, MI: Eerdmans, 1995), 59.

Isaiah 6 in order to see how verses 11–13 conclude the passage and how these verses could contribute to the idea so far observed and how this relates to the modern church. In response to the scorching message of judgment for idolatry in verses 9 and 10, Isaiah asks God how long this blinding and deafening judgment will last, and God's answer gives the effect and the extent of the judgment on Israel: "Until cities are devastated and without inhabitant, houses are without people, and the land is utterly desolate" (6:11b).

The divine response initially is that this ironic punishment will last until the land undergoes a severe devastation (6:11–12). Part of the ironic punishment is that not only will the idolaters become spiritually destroyed within their own beings, but their land will become "devastated" and "utterly desolate" as an outer reflection of the people's inner spiritual desolation. Even the cities and houses of the Israelites will become empty "without inhabitant" and "without people" to indicate further their judgment and the emptiness of their spiritual condition.

The extent of the judgment continues in Isaiah 6:12: "The LORD has removed men far away, and the forsaken places are many in the midst of the land." What was implied in verse 11 becomes explicit in verse 12: God will remove the inhabitants of Israel's land and send them into exile in another land. Israel's physical exile and separation from their promised land indicates their spiritual exile from God, since their land was where God's unique, special revelatory presence dwelt in the temple, which represented God's presence with his people through the priestly mediation and their worship. It is this idea that is presumably, to some degree, operative under the surface here. Israel's spiritual separation from God due to their intractable idolatry is partly pictured by their removal from that land where God said he would be intimately present with his people. This is not only a picture of their spiritual condition but a judgment for it.

Isaiah 6:13 explains the effect of Israel's spiritual and physical destruction and exile. God will make the nation completely spiritually insensitive so that they will be judged. It will be a thorough judgment. In verse 13 Isaiah announces yet again that God will judge Israel, even when they return from the judgment of exile, by making them become like their idols and thus to be ruined. The idea here is true with Israel and even us: what we revere, we resemble, either for restoration or ruin.

> Yet there will be a tenth portion in it [the land of Israel],
> And it will again be subject to burning,
> Like a terebinth or an oak
> Whose stump remains when it is felled.
> The holy seed is its stump. (Isa. 6:13)

A remnant ("a tenth portion") will survive from among those who remained living in the land and those from the judgment of exile. Will these survivors be repentant and faithful in response to the severe judgment narrated in verses 9–12? Most commentators think that the representation of the remnant as "subject to burning" like trees with a remaining "stump" indicates a positive picture of Israel, a picture of purification or refining of faithful Israel. It is more likely, however, that this, indeed, is not a positive picture.

First, the metaphor of trees burning is not a positive one in Isaiah. Elsewhere in the book the picture of oaks and terebinths burning is included in a description of God's destruction of idols. In particular, Isaiah 1:29–31 contains the only other use of "terebinth" in the book outside of 6:13. This unique parallelism is heightened by the observation that "burn" appears in close relation to "terebinth" in both passages. In Isaiah 1:29–31 these words appear as part of a description of Israel being judged by God because of their idolatry:

Surely you will be ashamed of the oaks which you have
>   desired,
And you will be embarrassed at the gardens which you have
>   chosen.
For you will be like [a terebinth] whose leaf fades away,
Or as a garden that has no water.
The strong man will become tinder,
His work also a spark.
Thus they shall both burn together,
And there will be none to quench them.

First, notice that those who worship in the idolatrous gardens (where ancient trees were revered and thought to possess divine spirits) will become as spiritually dry as those spiritually dry gardens; those who worship terebinth trees will spiritually fade away as the leaves of those trees will eventually fade away and die. Again, Israel is pictured as becoming like her idols. Additionally, the things that are burnt in the four lines of verse 31 ("the strong man" and "his work [of idols]") are most plausibly the subjects of verses 29 and 30—the idolaters and their idols ("trees which you have desired" and "gardens which you have chosen"). This identification, then, of the burning of both the idol worshipers and their idols follows naturally from the identification of the unfruitful spiritual condition of the idolaters with that of their idols in verses 29 and 30. In Isaiah 1:29–31, it is said not only that Israel would "be like a terebinth whose leaf fades away" but also that the nation and their terebinths would "both burn together."

The same application of this "burning terebinth" metaphor likely occurs also in Isaiah 6:13, especially because of the proximity of the two contexts. Therefore, in both Isaiah 6:13 and 1:29–31 rebellious Israel is portrayed as becoming "like" the idols ("idolatrous trees") that they worshiped. Israel will become like these trees, resembling their destructive destiny, an expression of the ironic principle in Psalms 115:8 and 135:18. Just as their idolatrous trees would be burned, so the idolatrous Israelites are twice spoken of as idolatrous trees being burned. Along with the literal physical destruction of the idolatrous objects will be the spiritual destruction of those who worshiped them, though in some cases they would also be physically destroyed.

The Hebrew word for "stump" at the end of Isaiah 6:13a never means stump in any of the other numerous times that the word is used in the Old Testament.[4] The majority of the time, it refers to an idolatrous pillar as an object of worship (though sometimes it can have a positive meaning, to commemorate something). That it refers to an idol here is apparent from noticing that elsewhere when the word occurs together with "oak" or "tree," it usually refers to an idolatrous object. The connection noticed between Isaiah 1:29–31 and Isaiah 6:13a confirms that the stump is part of an idolatrous tree that has undergone destruction.

Isaiah 6:13b, then, is asserting that the nation that Yahweh intended to be a "holy seed" (Israel) had become so profane through idolatry that it was indistinguishable from the idolatrous nations. The radical but not unprecedented conclusion of verse 13b, that even the remnant (the tenth) "holy seed" had become idolatrous, signals the end of Israel's traditionally understood theocratic existence. The only other occurrence of "holy seed" in the Old Testament is in Ezra 9:1–2, where the phrase is negative and refers to Israel as "the holy seed" who has intermarried with pagan idol worshipers and followed their idolatrous abominations, which further supports the same negative notion of "holy seed" in Isaiah 6:13b.

---

4. In both of its variant feminine forms.

The purpose of the similar portrayals of Israel as burning, idolatrous trees in Isaiah 1:29–31 and 6:13 is to link their judgment to idolatry in order to emphasize that their punishment was due to their idol worship. What a fitting retributive irony that those "who inflame [themselves] among the [idolatrous] oaks" (Isa. 57:5) would have their judgment described as trees being set to flame!

In summary, the expressions describing Israel as having ears but not hearing (6:9–10) and like a burning tree (Isa. 6:13a) are best understood as metaphors of idolatry that are applied to the disobedient nation in order to emphasize that they would be punished for their idol worship by being judged in the same manner as their idols, i.e., by being destroyed. An aspect of this pronouncement of judgment also includes the idea that the idolaters had begun to resemble the nature of their idols—they had become as spiritually lifeless as their idols.[5] Israel thought that worshiping idols would lead to happiness and fulfillment, but it led ironically to the opposite—sadness and emptiness. This idea of resembling what you revere for ruin is a part of retributive irony and permeates Scripture and forms a biblical theology of idolatry. But its opposite, resembling what you revere for restoration (as in the case of the prophet Isaiah), is a part of restorative irony, which also streams throughout the Bible.

Conclusion and Further Application

What you revere, you resemble, either for restoration or ruin. What Israel revered, they resembled for their ruin. What Isaiah revered, he resembled for his restoration. And the same is true with us.

It is interesting that Isaiah 6:9–10 is quoted in the New Testament by all the Gospel writers at decisive points in their accounts of Christ

---

5. For an in-depth argument supporting the interpretation of Isaiah 6 in this chapter, see G. K. Beale, "Isaiah 6:9–13: A Retributive Taunt against Idolatry," 257–78; and Beale, *We Become What We Worship*, 36–70.

(Matt. 13; Mark 4; Luke 4; and John 12). It was put there to say that the generation of Israelites living at Jesus's time were going to be finally judged because they idolized tradition. There was going to be a reconstitution of the nation on the basis of one individual, Jesus. Note the formula of "hearing" in Matthew 13 (2x), which is rooted in Isaiah 6:9 (cf. Ezek. 3:27 ["He who hears, let him hear"] as part of the allusion in Matthew 13 [Matt. 13:9, 43]).

Isaiah 40–66 has the same theme as this very pessimistic note here at the end of Isaiah 6. But Isaiah prophesies a new root of Jesse in 11:1. A root will spring up from that stump. It will be Jesus, and there will be a new Israel constituted on a new basis, not on the old theocratic basis. But Isaiah says in chapter 66:18–21 that even Gentiles will be made priests in this new Israel. It is not a total rejection of ethnic Jews. However, there will be ethnic Jews together with Gentiles in this new reconstituted nation. Acts ends by quoting Isaiah 6:9–10 to talk about the reconstitution of new Israel, the rejection of the ethnic nation, and the reconstitution of a new nation.

How does this apply to us? At the end of each of the letters in Revelation, all addressed to Gentile churches, five of those seven churches are in danger of losing their Christian identity because of idol worship. Each letter concludes with, "He who has an ear, let him hear" (2:7, 11, 17, 29; 3:6, 13, 22). This is an exhortation to genuine believers. They are in danger of losing their identity as the people of God and as God's local churches because they are idolaters. They are coming under the anesthesia of idolatry. They need to be shocked out of it (and note that the expression "If anyone has an ear, let him hear" in Revelation 13:9 and its context explicitly underscore the idolatry theme of worshiping the beast). Those confessing believers among the churches addressed who do not respond positively to this exhortation prove themselves to have become intractably deaf and blind on a spiritual level.

It is true not only on the national level of Israel and the corporate level of the church but on the individual level as well. What do you resemble? Is it some aspect of the world? Second Corinthians 10:5 says that we are to take "every thought captive to the obedience of Christ." Any thought that we do not subject to the rule of Christ is an idolatrous thought.

Thoughts about getting married are sometimes not brought under the sovereignty of Christ. People do not always evaluate a prospective spouse in terms of his or her commitment to the Lord. In such cases, they tend to focus on good looks and personality. When you marry someone on that basis, you risk experiencing the same thing that happened to King Solomon (see 1 Kings 11). He married idolatrous women from the pagan nations, whom God had commanded the Israelites not to marry lest the Israelites be influenced to become idol worshipers. Solomon not only built for his wives altars for their idols, but he worshiped their idols along with them. His commitment to his wives was not based on his commitment to God, and so his marital commitments were idolatrous. Whatever we commit ourselves to, we often become like, and Solomon began to resemble the ungodly character of his wives and, thus, worshiped their idols and became as unspiritual as his wives and their idols. His great wisdom did not influence them, but their ungodliness influenced him. Overemphasizing appearance, someone's pretty eyes and ears, may result in our own spiritual eyes and ears becoming dead in our relationships with others.

This is true also with peer groups. If you are a Christian, and you are in middle school or high school or college, how do you relate to various groups of friends? To be accepted by the group of which you want to be a part, do you have to become like the group in ways that would be displeasing to your Lord? Maybe there are pressures to participate in drug use or excessive use of alcohol or in sexual immorality; or perhaps to be considered "cool" you are expected to use profanity the way the rest of the group does or to engage in some illegal activity such as theft or vandalism. If you resemble the group in these or other ways displeasing to God, it means that you are committed to pleasing the group more than God. Your peer group has become an idol. Do you find your true identity with God or with your social group? This is what the psalmist prays about in Psalm 119:133–134:

> Establish my footsteps in Your word,
> And do not let any iniquity have dominion over me.
> Redeem me from the oppression of man [i.e., from the world]
> That I may keep Your precepts.

Romans 12:2 says, "Do not be conformed to this world, but be transformed by the renewing of your mind [in Scripture], so that you may prove what the will of God is, that which is good and acceptable and perfect."

Again, the principle is this: what you revere, you resemble, either for ruin or restoration. To commit yourself to some part of the creation more than to the Creator is idolatry. And like Israel, when you worship something of this earth, you become like it—spiritually lifeless and insensitive to God as a piece of wood, rock, and stone.[6] You become spiritually blind, deaf, and dumb even though you still have eyes and ears physically. To the extent that you commit yourself to something that does not have God's Spirit, to that degree you will be unspiritual.

Jeremiah 2:2 says that Israel worshiped vain and empty idols and became vain and empty. Our lives become vain and empty when we commit to idols of this world. The Hebrew words for idols are significant in this respect. The meaning of one of these words is a "hurtful, painful thing." Another word for idol in the Old Testament can be

---

6. See Beale, *We Become What We Worship*, for this ironic theme throughout the Old Testament and the New Testament.

translated as "nonexistent thing." You may commit yourself to some earthly idol for fulfillment, but there will be no fulfillment from it.

When you begin to resemble the idols of the world and spiritual harm is set in motion, you don't often feel the harm at first. Often you don't sense it until it is too late. You are anesthetized to the hurt for a while—you have eyes but can't see. If you do not come out from under the anesthesia, then much harm can be done to you before it becomes apparent. You need to be shocked out of the anesthesia by God's word. Thus we must come to God's word continually to be continually shocked out of our spiritual anesthesia.

So Isaiah is telling us that Israel revered idols, became like them—spiritually insensitive—and that likeness led to their ruin. What we revere, we resemble, either for ruin or restoration.

If we trust in the Lord and commit ourselves to him, if we do not conform ourselves to the world, as Romans 12:2 says, but are transformed and committed to Jesus Christ, we will begin to resemble the image of God in which we were originally created. Likewise 2 Corinthians 3:18 9 (ESV) says:

> We all with unveiled face, beholding the glory of the Lord, are being transformed into the same image from one degree of glory to another. For this comes from the Lord who is the Spirit.

All of us are imitators, and there is no spiritual neutrality. If you think that you can be spiritually neutral, you are wrong. You are being conformed either to an idol of the world in some way or to God. I used to think that Christians could be spiritually neutral. I would not read the Bible or pray for a few weeks, and all that time, in reality, I was subtly being conformed to something besides God's word.

We can know if we are idol worshipers if we claim to be true Christians but do not consistently put Christ first above all other things. If not putting Christ first in one's life is the bent of a person's lifestyle, then such people should have no assurance that they are really Christians. This can be true of businesspeople, students, wives, husbands, and children. This can even be true of seminary students; some have found halfway through their seminary education that they were not Christians after all. Even ministers have become converted in the midst of their own ministries. If you commit to something consistently other than to the Lord and his word, it may be, as John is saying to the churches, you are on the verge of losing your Christian identity, and it may mean that you never were a Christian at all. Yet if you heed that very perilous warning not to worship idols lest you lose your Christian identity, the warning will be the very means by which you maintain your Christian identity.

Solomon was apparently redeemed, but he was a partial idol worshiper, which led to his hurt. There were times in Solomon's life that he should have had no assurance of being a true believer in the Lord. In order to discern if we are becoming idolaters, we should first ask ourselves whether we spend time consistently in God's word, meditating on it, and in prayer. Do we have a time of Bible reading every day? The lack of such a time may be one indication of idolatry. If we do not regularly practice these activities, then we are not setting God before our eyes consistently, and it is more likely that we will commit ourselves to something in the world other than God.

As we noted, the apostle Paul instructs us to bring every thought captive to the thinking of Jesus Christ. What corner of our lives are we not relating to Christ? Is it a dating or marriage relationship? Is it some aspect concerning our children, perhaps a failure to devote sufficient time to guide them in spiritual instruction? All of us to some degree, until the age of perfection, until we reach heaven, want to glorify ourselves. Is that why we do the things we do? Do we want glory for what we do? When people praise you for doing well, do you give God the credit, or do you take it for yourself? Why do you love praise for what you do? Are you really taking pleasure in what God takes pleasure in—his glory?

If we want to be committed to him, it's worth asking whether we idolize our schedule. Do we work God around our schedule, or do we fit our schedule around God? We need to see all of life through the lens of the Scriptures, not to be conformed to the world but to be transformed to Christ. Some people have their schedule as an idol in order to worship the larger idol of money.

What we revere is what we resemble, either for ruin or restoration. May we revere the Lord in his word and resemble him for our restoration in redemption and not revere the world and resemble it for our ruin. May God be with us as the true, new Israel to worship him, and may we not worship idols as Israel of old did.

3

The Irony of Salvation

So far we have observed primarily the retributive irony experienced by those who try sinfully to obtain blessings in this life but receive only cursings, either in the here and now or ultimately in the hereafter. However, there is a flip side to this ironic coin. There is also the irony whereby the faithful who try to pursue godliness and justice seem only to be cursed in this life. Nevertheless, Scripture asserts of such saints that even if they appear to be cursed on the earthly level, they still possess spiritual blessings both in the present and for eternity. In other words, the ironic principle associated with the lives of faithful believers is that you can't judge a book by its cover. That is, adversity, affliction, or failure in everyday life is no indicator of the nature of a person's heart and relationship with God. We may call this "restorative irony."

Sometimes (perhaps often) Christians do not enjoy material abundance, but after death they will receive the consummative eternal blessing of salvation through Christ. Occasionally believers are granted success during their earthly sojourn, and it often comes after long periods of failure and calamity. Such enjoyment of prosperity is given by God as a foreshadowing or token of the grander blessings to be gained in eternity or as a vindication of the persecuted sufferer, pointing to his ultimate vindication in Christ. So either in the present or after death, God is always at work for his people, ironically turning their evil into good, their cursings into blessings, their temporal adversity into eternal prosperity. This principle of restorative irony, of course, applies to the very beginning of the Christian life. One becomes a Christian through God's transforming the sinful heart of unbelief into a heart of repentance and faith so that a person's impending curse of damnation is turned into a blessing of eternal salvation.

Again, contemporary illustrations are at hand to illustrate the principle of redemptive irony. The atheist activist Madalyn Murray O'Hair was almost a household name in the 1980s. She labored to thwart the influence of Christianity in our culture. Initially, she first attracted nationwide attention when she claimed that her atheistic son should not be required to sit through Bible reading and prayer in a public school classroom. Her son, William Murray, was the defendant in the 1963 historic lawsuit in which the US Supreme Court concluded that prayer in public school was unconstitutional. The O'Hair household was perhaps (it is hoped) not typical. William was raised as an atheist in a home full of constant violence and profanity. From a biblical perspective, William's life was leaning in the same blasphemous and unbelieving direction as his mother's, especially after the historic trial. As he grew up, he twice married and divorced, abused the women in his life, became involved with drugs, and could not hold down a steady job. He was on the road to spiritual disaster, doom, and judgment. Then in his thirties he experienced a turn-around. He came to believe there is a God because he had come to believe in the devil, since he had seen evidence of him in his mother. Apparently, he became a Christian. The one who helped outlaw prayer in the schools because of his atheism became an avowed theist and man of prayer. The apparent curse of his early upbringing was turned ironically into a blessing by God. And his mother, whose goal it had been to cause many to lose their faith, lost her own son to the faith.[1] God had accomplished a good, redemptive purpose out of the evil designs of this ungodly mother. Although young O'Hair's conversion was from radical atheism, all conversions illustrate to varying degrees the irony involved in his experience.

We could recount many conversion stories of those whose conversion appeared most unlikely. Augustine, one of the most influential Christian theologians of church history (AD 354–430), spent the first thirty-two years of his life as an unbeliever. He lived with a mistress for fifteen of those years, who bore him an illegitimate son. During much of this time he felt that one could not have intellectual integrity and also be a Christian. However, his real problem was a moral one, as he enjoyed indulging in the sexual lusts of the flesh. Yet he became a Christian at the age of thirty-two while reading Romans 13:13–14: "Let us behave properly . . . not in sexual promiscuity and sensuality. . . . But put on the Lord Jesus Christ, and make no provision for the flesh in regard to its lusts." God not only reversed his unbelief to belief but caused him to become one of the greatest theologians of the church.

Interestingly, one of the main biblical words for *conversion* in Scripture is *repentance*, which literally means "to turn" one's mind and life from unbelief and sin in the opposite direction, to faith and righteousness. Although humans are repeatedly commanded "to turn" (repent), they are unable because of their bondage to Satan, sin, and the flesh (cf. Rom. 3:10–12; 2 Cor. 4:4; Eph. 2:1–3, 5; 2 Tim. 2:25–26). Only God has the power to turn one's heart to himself, to cause light to "shine out of darkness" (2 Cor. 4:6; see also Acts 3:26;

---

1. This synopsis of William Murray's life is based on an article, "O'Hair Son Still Preaching against Her," in *Pittsburgh Press*, September 6, 1982, 8.

5:31; 11:18; 2 Tim. 2:25). So the psalmist appropriately prays, "O God of hosts, restore us, and cause Your face to shine upon us, and we will be saved" (Ps. 80:3, 7, 19). God alone can reverse a person's depraved one-track mind, leading to hell, and transfer that person to a heavenward road. God is always at work ironically transforming cursing into blessing, darkness into light, and unbelief into belief. One of the most striking examples is what happened to Adam and Eve.

Another Look at the Fall by the Tree in Eden

Earlier we saw that God created Adam and Eve to resemble his image, but they sinned by disobeying God's word and came to resemble the serpent's sinful and deceptive character. This resulted in their judgment. Because of their sin, they incurred spiritual death immediately and physical death subsequently. However, whereas Satan's judgment was irreversible (see Gen. 3:14–15), the first couple were not to be left in their condition of spiritual death and alienation from God.

Before discussing the ultimate blessing that God would cause to arise from the first couple's curse, we need to review in more depth the original threefold purpose of Adam in the garden of Eden in order to see how he failed and for what he was cursed. First, Adam was to perform a priestly function. To him was imparted God's word, which he was held responsible to mediate to his wife (Gen. 2:16–17). In addition to being priestly custodian of God's *torah*, Adam was also to be guardian of God's edenic sanctuary. Adam was placed in the garden not merely to till it but also to guard it from anything unclean that might enter (Gen. 2:15). The Hebrew word for "guard," also translated as "cultivate" or "keep," is used elsewhere in the Old Testament for priests who guard God's sanctuary (cf. Gen. 3:24; Num. 1:53; 3:8, 32; 8:26; 18:3ff; 31:30, 47; Zech. 3:7), so this is likely how God's command to guard the garden is to be understood. Genesis 2:15 says that God placed Adam in the garden "to cultivate [i.e., work] it and keep it." The two Hebrew words for "cultivate" and "keep" are usually translated "serve" and "guard" (or "keep") elsewhere in the Old Testament. It is true that the Hebrew word usually translated "cultivate" can refer to an agricultural task when used by itself (e.g., Gen. 2:5; 3:23). When, however, these two words in Hebrew (verbal and nominal forms) occur closely together in the Old Testament, they refer either to Israelites "serving" God and "guarding [keeping]" God's word (approximately ten times) or to priests who "keep" the "service" (or "charge") of the tabernacle (see Num. 3:7–8; 8:25–26; 18:5–6; 1 Chron. 23:32; Ezek. 44:14). The latter is likely in mind in Genesis 2:15. Even if "cultivate" for the first Hebrew word is the best translation, which is quite plausible, it would have to do with a priestly caretaking of the garden.[2]

The symbolic meaning of the tree of the knowledge of good and evil (Gen. 2:17) explains how Adam was to guard the garden. Throughout the rest of Scripture, the skill of discerning between good and evil belongs to kings or judges who are qualified to render legal verdicts or judgments (2 Sam. 14:17; 1 Kings 3:9, 28). In this light, it may be concluded that Adam was to exercise his priestly duty by discriminating between evil and good and keeping the former from entering the garden sanctuary. The tree could be understood as the judgment seat where such decisions were to be formally pronounced. When Satan would question God's word at this tree, Adam would be forced to discern between good and evil, and it would be his guardian role to pronounce judgment on the evil serpent and expel him from the holy sanctuary.

The second purpose of Adam involved a kingly function. He was commanded to "rule over . . . all the earth" (Gen. 1:26) and to "subdue . . . and rule over . . . every living thing that moves on the earth"—even

---

2. See G. K. Beale, *The Temple and the Church's Mission*, New Studies in Biblical Theology 17 (Leicester, UK: Inter-Varsity Press, 2004), 66–69. That Adam was a priest is also apparent from observing that Ezek. 28:12–13, 18 portrays him in the sanctuary of Eden wearing clothing with the same jewels that were on the clothing of Israel's high priest (Ex. 28:17–20).

over serpents (see Gen. 1:28). Adam was the divine ambassador commissioned to rule the earth under God's authority and on his behalf.

Adam's third purpose on earth focused on family obligations.
Adam was to be the head of his household, as implied by his being
created first and by the naming of his wife, as he had expressed his
leadership of the animals by naming them.[3] These latter two offices
should probably be seen as aspects of his priestly duty: he was to
rule the earth for God's glory, and his leadership of his family was to
be expressed primarily by mediating God's word to his wife so that
she also could serve and obey the Lord with him (see Gen. 2:16–17).
Hence Adam was a priestly guardian not only of the garden sanctuary of God but also of the earth and of his family.[4]

Against the background of Adam's obligations, it can be seen that
his fall involved much more than merely the sin of eating forbidden
fruit. Meredith Kline has explained the essence of Adam's sin:

> God had brought Satan to the judgment tree to be damned. To
> man had been assigned the awesome role of standing as God's
> vice-regent at the place of judgment and consigning the great
> adversary to perdition.... Man, however, had utterly failed....
> He had declared good to be evil and evil to be good.[5]

Adam failed in his priestly role of guarding the garden sanctuary by
not discerning the wickedness of the serpent, by not pronouncing
his judgment at the tree, and by not casting the vile snake into the
outer darkness beyond the garden's confines. Because Adam did not
judge the serpent, he himself was judged by God. Just as unbelievers

---

3. With respect to Adam's headship over Eve in Gen. 2:22 see James Hurley, *Man and Woman in Biblical Perspective* (Grand Rapids, MI: Zondervan, 1981), 206–13.

4. This summary of Adam's pre-fall responsibilities is based on Meredith G. Kline's *Kingdom Prologue: Genesis Foundations for a Covenantal Worldview* (Overland Park, KS: Two Age Press, 2000), 125–29, 161–63.

5. Kline, *Kingdom Prologue*, 178–79.

will hide from the presence of the Lamb at his second coming (Rev. 6:15–16), so Adam and Eve "hid themselves from the presence of the LORD God" as he entered the garden to judge them (Gen. 3:8).[6] Not only was Adam's delinquent judgment of Satan ironically turned into his own judgment, but now he who had been commissioned by God to "subdue and rule over everything that moves on the earth" was subdued and ruled over by the creeping serpent, to whom Adam had delivered his crown. And he who was to rule and subdue "all the earth" was subdued by the earth,[7] as he would "return to the ground" because of the death curse now imposed upon him (Gen. 2:19). Adam's only crown after the fall was one composed of both thorns and thistles and the sweat of his face (Gen. 3:18–19).

The fall occurred also because Adam was led by his wife rather than leading her, as he should have, being the priestly guardian of his household. In consequence of inverting the order of the family, God cursed Adam by proclaiming that henceforth his wife would continually desire to rule over him (cf. Gen. 3:16 and 4:7), the very reverse of his intended design for her. By usurping her husband's headship, the woman, who was originally appointed to be a minister of life to the man, ironically became a minister of death.

However, all these ironies of judgment upon Adam were ultimately to be reversed. This reversal is already intimated in Genesis 3:15–21, where Adam is both cursed with death (v. 19) but also given the promise that God will transform his curse into the blessing of life. This reversal of Adam's destiny is first indicated in Genesis 3:15, where God promises that a future descendant of the woman will defeat the serpent who had enslaved Adam and Eve with death: "He [the woman's seed] shall bruise you [the serpent] on the head." She was named Eve, which means "life," because of this future descendant

---

6. This observation is made by Kline, *Kingdom Prologue*, 182.

7. Kline, *Kingdom Prologue*, 189.

from her womb. Her future seed would reverse the curse of death into life. Thus the woman who had delivered man to sin would also deliver to him a savior; the woman, who was originally to be a minister of life to the man but became a minister of death, was transformed back to her original role as minister of life by bearing the Prince of life, the Messiah.[8] In this regard, Warren Austin Gage has noted:

> The man and the woman are subjects of grace as well as wrath, and the prophetic oracle contains a pronouncement as well of restorative irony. There had been demonic irony that the woman whose life was derived from man should become to him the minister of death. But there is divine irony in the appointing of the woman to be the mother of all living (Gen. 3:20).[9]

Significantly, a number of Old Testament scholars have asserted that the Hebrew name Eve (*ḥawwâ*), which means "life," was derived from an ancient word meaning "serpent" (cf. the Aramaic word *ḥawwê*, as well as the similar word in Syriac and Arabic). But what does the idea of *life* have in common with that of *serpent*? The Genesis 3 context especially seems to affirm not only that the two meanings are not associated but that they are really opposite, for the serpent caused Eve's death, not her life. Therefore, Hebrew scholars have puzzled over the connection of the name Eve ("life") with that of "serpent" and have not discovered how the concepts could be linked in Genesis 3.

However, in light of our discussion so far, could it be that the linking of the two meanings expresses an ironic intent? The main thesis of the narrative in Genesis 3:14–21 is that God is planning not merely to judge but subsequently to convert man's curse of death into

---

8. This irony involving the woman's role was suggested in unpublished comments by W. A. Gage.

9. W. A. Gage, *The Gospel of Genesis: Studies in Protology and Eschatology* (Winona Lake, WI: Eisenbrauns, 1984), 66.

life. Therefore, death and life are integrally related in that the latter is to arise ironically from the former, according to divine design. Would not such an irony be intensified through assigning to the woman the name "life," which etymologically originated from an archaic word meaning "serpent," the author of her death? Who knows in the linguistic history of the ancient Near Eastern languages how the Hebrews developed their word for *life* from a word for *serpent*? But the appropriateness of choosing this word with which to rename the woman certainly appears well suited narratively to emphasize the idea that the serpent's death curse upon the first couple was already in process of being transformed into a divine life blessing.

Renaming may even have been a way to mock the serpent himself; all the serpent's efforts to bring about the death of man led ultimately only to man's life through the life-giving efforts of the Prince of Life, Eve's messianic seed. Perhaps because of this connection of the serpent with life in the beginning of history, the serpent became a traditional divine symbol of life in pagan religions that developed subsequently (note also the symbol of the serpent even for our contemporary medical profession).

That the curse of damnation on Adam and Eve was already in the process of being turned into a blessing of salvation is evident from Genesis 3:21: "The LORD God made garments of skin for Adam and his wife, and clothed them." Many commentators have recognized in these words the implication that God had shed animals' blood in order to clothe Adam and Eve with skins and that this could be seen as sacrificed blood that covered over their sin. This first animal sacrifice has also been seen as an anticipation of the Passover lamb sacrifice subsequently celebrated annually on the Day of Atonement in Israel, and it has also been viewed as a foreshadowing of God's sacrificial lamb, Jesus Christ, at the cross.

The First Adam and the Last Adam

The curse upon the first Adam was taken away by the last Adam, Jesus Christ. Paul explains that the first Adam "is a type [or foreshadowing] of Him [Christ] who was to come" (Rom. 5:14). But how could sinful Adam be a prophetic pointer of the coming perfect Adam? Such a comparison seems blasphemous. What does Paul then have in mind?

Before understanding the comparison, we need to come to grips with what Paul means by "type." We have already suggested that *type* has to do with the idea of "prophetic shadowing." In the Old Testament there are two kinds of prophecy. First, there is direct verbal prediction, which is what most people understand as the only sort of prophecy in the Bible. This kind of prophecy is found in Isaiah 53, which verbally foretold in detail how the Messiah would suffer as a penal substitute for his sinful people. The same phenomenon occurs in Micah 5:2 where in straightforward words Bethlehem is prophesied to be the Messiah's birthplace.

However, a second kind of prophecy in Scripture is referred to as "indirect typological prophecy." This is prophecy conveyed not through words but through historical events involving people or things that correspond to and foreshadow events in the New Testament. For example, the Passover lamb was a prophetic foreshadowing of Jesus's lamb-like sacrifice at the cross; the exodus deliverance of Israel from Egyptian bondage was an adumbration of the Christian's deliverance from the bondage of sin by Christ's death. In fact, the prophets, priests, and kings of Israel all imperfectly foreshadowed Jesus Christ, who would perfectly combine all three offices into his one person.

Therefore, Paul is saying in Romans 5:14 that, indeed, the first Adam was a typological prophecy of Christ. Paul explains how, in Romans 5:17–19:

For if by the transgression of the one, death reigned through the one, much more those who receive the abundance of grace and of the gift of righteousness will reign in life through the One, Jesus Christ. So then as through one transgression there resulted condemnation to all men, even so through one act of righteousness there resulted justification of life to all men. For as through the one man's disobedience the many were made sinners, even so through the obedience of the One the many will be made righteous.

For Paul, Adam was not the only foreshadowing of Christ, but more shockingly, it was the event of the fall itself that contained a prophetic pattern of the event of Christ's death. That is, Adam's transgression and disobedience through which the many were made sinners and which resulted in condemnation and death for all, was a prefigurement of the last Adam's one act of righteousness and obedience through which the many will be made righteous and which resulted in justification and life for all. The fall, then, was a typological event that ironically prophesied how the disobedience, condemnation, and death set in motion by the first Adam would be reversed into obedience, justification, and life through the work of the last Adam. Adam's curse of death on the hill of Eden (cf. Ezek. 28:13–14) was itself a predictive pointer to Christ's blessing of life regained for man on the hill of Calvary. This was an ironic prophetic pattern since it prefigured the opposite of what was to happen at the cross.

Even the sacraments of the Christian faith memorialize this transformative irony of how Eden's damnation was turned into Calvary's salvation. Just as Adam's eating was a means of his death, so Christ inaugurated a ritual of eating to symbolize the means by which life can be gained (John 6:48–58; 1 Cor. 11; 23–29). Baptism likewise signifies the curse of death (descending into the water) and the overcoming of the curse through the resurrection from the dead (ascending out of the water;[10] see Rom. 6:4).

Adam's tree appeared to lead to life and glory but ended up leading to death and disrepute. On the other hand, Christ's tree appeared to lead to death and ill repute but resulted in life and glorification. Paul succinctly summarizes this ironic reversal: Christ became "a curse for us— for it is written, 'Cursed is everyone who hangs on a tree'—in order that in Christ Jesus the blessing of Abraham might come" (Gal. 3:13–14).

A Mighty Fortress Is Our God

We have seen in Genesis 3:15 that the serpent was destined for fatal defeat by some future descendant of Eve, whom we have identified as Jesus Christ. Indeed, Jesus Christ himself is the prime example of one whose death was turned back into life, whose defeat was turned into victory.

However, in early Old Testament times the precise manner by which Eve's messianic seed would defeat the serpent was not clear. Nevertheless, there were historical events that illustrated the ironic principle by which satanic evil would be vanquished. One of the clearest pictures of this principle is seen in David's defeat of Goliath. During the reign of Saul, Israel was at war with the Philistines. A giant named Goliath stepped forward to challenge the strongest Israelite warrior in battle, and the outcome would determine victory at a national level. No one in Israel took up the challenge, but they "fled from him and were greatly afraid" (1 Sam. 17:24). David's older brothers were among the army of Israel, and he had been sent by his father to bring them food and refreshment. Having heard Goliath's taunt, David angrily exclaimed that this "uncircumcised Philistine" (v. 26) was not worthy to challenge God's army, and he offered to fight Goliath himself. His older brothers ridiculed him, and Saul said he

---

10. For this sacramental irony see Gage, *The Gospel of Genesis*, 60.

was too young. Indeed, David was but a young lad (not old enough to fight in the army), and Goliath was a giant and an experienced warrior. He was about 10 feet tall and his armor weighed approximately 125 pounds, probably almost the sum total of David's weight.

David approached the giant with no armor or weapons except a slingshot with small stones. Goliath "cursed David by his gods" (v. 43) because of David's apparently stupid presumptuousness. David responded, "You come to me with a sword, a spear, and a javelin, but I come to you in the name of the LORD of hosts" (v. 45). Through David's faith, God ironically caused strength to come from his youthful weakness in order to conquer the strong giant. David killed Goliath with but one small stone in his slingshot.

This story well illustrates the ironic principle by which the Messiah would overcome his enemy. David himself sets forth in Psalm 8 one of the earliest Old Testament hints about the Messiah's method in achieving victory. Although David does not mention the cross or resurrection or even suffering, he insinuates that the victory will not be won through physical strength. David begins the psalm by proclaiming about the Lord:

How majestic is Your name in all the earth,
Who have displayed Your splendor above the heavens! (v. 1)

God is glorified through the earth, and the splendor of this earthly creation outshines even his divine handiwork in the heavens. Someone has said that verse 1 portrays the picture of the earth as a jewel in the setting of the universe. That the emphasis in verse 1 is upon the earth more than the heavens glorifying God is evident from the last verse of the psalm: "How majestic is Your name in all the earth!" (v. 9).

In 8:2 something is identified in the earth that makes God's name majestic:

> From the mouth of infants and nursing babes You have
>   established strength,
> Because of Your adversaries,
> To make the enemy and the revengeful cease.

"Infants" and "nursing babes" are figures of speech denoting weakness. God has appointed what is weakest in creation to display its greatest strength and to vanquish the forces of evil. Such an ironic display of strength through weakness gives more honor to God's name than anything else, primarily because, in this way, Satan's forces are finally to be thwarted. Ironic weakness is emphasized in the Aramaic version of Psalm 8 (called the Targum),[11] where in the last part of verse 2 this paradoxical strength is said to "destroy the author of enmity and the violent one"—that is, Satan. The finality of this victory is stressed through a literal rendering of the Hebrew in verse 2: "to make the enemy and revengeful have a sabbath [or rest]." God's enemies will be "put to rest" permanently. As mentioned, David's defeat of Goliath may have been a precursor of such a future victory, since it well illustrated strength coming from a weak child in overcoming the archenemy of God's people (cf. 1 Sam. 17:1–49).[12]

In verses 3 and 4 David compares the massive heavens with the weakness of God's earthly creation, humanity, and says that seemingly the former would be more significant to God, but in reality he deems humanity as more important:

> When I consider Your heavens, the work of Your fingers,
> The moon and the stars, which You have ordained;
> What is man, that You take thought of him?
> And the son of man that You care for him?

---

11. The Targum was the Aramaic translation of the Old Testament used by the Jews during synagogue worship in the first century AD.

12. The 1 Samuel background has been noticed by Gage, *Gospel of Genesis*, 66.

Man appears to be identified with the weakness of verse 2 that will defeat the forces of wickedness. As generally stated in verse 1, the human aspect of the earthly creation is again said to outshine the glory of the heavenly creation. Against the backdrop of the starry host, man appears weak and insignificant, but God cares for him more than any other part of the universe and has planned that, somehow, man will express the greatest strength of it. This is the expected positive answer to the rhetorical questions asked in verse 4. Interestingly, "the son of man" here (v. 4) is viewed as the theological center of the universe.

But how does God pay special attention to humanity, and in what way is humanity more important that the rest of creation? So far, the answer is that God has singled out weak humanity from all of creation and purposed to defeat the strength of evil. In verses 5–8, humanity's victory over evil is developed and stated in a more positive form. Although the man in this psalm appears frail and unimportant, God has crowned him as king of all creation (v. 5: "Yet You . . . crown him with glory and majesty!"). His kingly rule is delineated in verses 6–8:[13]

> You make him to rule over the works of Your hands;
> You have put all things under his feet,
> All sheep and oxen,
> And also the beasts of the field,
> The birds of the heavens and the fish of the sea,
> Whatever passes through the paths of the seas.

Perhaps not coincidentally the Aramaic Old Testament used by the first-century Jews translated "Whatever passes through the paths of the seas" as "the Leviathan which passes along the paths of the seas." Possibly the theme of man's future defeat of evil from verse 2 is

---

13. The connection between v. 2 and vv. 3–8 in which Adam is linked with the weakness that overcomes evil in v. 2 was first suggested to me in a sermon by W. A. Gage, though I have found subsequent commentators who have made the link.

being alluded to again here, since Leviathan elsewhere in the Scripture is sometimes a symbol for Satan or that which is evil.[14]

Since the psalm is a *unity*, man's defeat of evil through weakness in verse 2 should be connected in some way with his rule over the whole created order in verses 5–8. Therefore, we ought to understand his rule in the latter part of the psalm in the light of verse 2. Weakness can also be discerned in verse 4 through the Hebrew word used for "man," since elsewhere in the Old Testament it usually refers to man in his *weakness*.[15] Therefore, the display of ruling power through weakness that brings most glory to God in his creation is the rationale causing David to conclude the psalm by exclaiming, "How majestic is Your name in all the earth!" (v. 9). The theme of Psalm 8 may then be stated this way: God's name is glorified throughout the universe because of the ironic earthly rule of the apparently weak son of man. He rules strongly through weakness.

Many commentators believe that the subject of Psalm 8 is the first Adam before the fall or mankind generally after the fall, since all people rule over the animal world. But this is a short-sighted view, since this would not explain sufficiently how the man *ironically* rules over creation, nor does it account for the man's defeat of evil through his weakness. Furthermore, we have already discussed above how Adam—and all subsequent people in him—*lost* dominion over creation because of sin and came into bondage to the creation itself (to the creeping serpent and to the ground). Consequently, the subject of this psalm cannot be Adam or mankind.

Who then is the grand subject of Psalm 8? The New Testament identifies the son of man (literally, son of Adam) in this psalm as Jesus Christ, who "destroyed the author of enmity and the violent one" (this is the

---

14. Ps. 74:14; Isa. 27:1; cf. Job 3:8; 41:1.
15. Three other Hebrew words could have been used here, but this is the only one that, when differing in meaning from the other words, connotes "man in his weakness."

paraphrase of the Hebrew by the Aramaic version of Ps. 8:2) through
the weakness at the cross. Nevertheless, verses 5–8 of the psalm are an
allusion to Genesis 1:26–30, which is God's commission to Adam and
Eve to have dominion over the earth. But this commission is now applied by Psalm 8 to a new man, or last Adam, to do that in which the
first failed—reign over the earth, including the creeping, satanic serpent.
Adam's son, the Son of Man, would be the one to reverse the devilish
curse imposed on his human father. Hebrews 2:6–8 quotes Psalm 8:4–7
and then applies those verses to Christ's death on the cross:

> But we do see Him who has been made for a little while lower
> than the angels [Ps. 8:5], namely, Jesus, because of the suf-
> fering of death crowned with glory and honor [Ps. 8:5], that
> . . . He might taste death for everyone. . . . Through death He
> might render powerless him who had the power of death, that
> is, the devil. (Heb. 2:9, 14)

Undoubtedly, the writer of Hebrews made the same connection
between Psalm 8:2 and 8:6–7 that we have also made so that he sees
God "establishing strength" [literally "a bulwark"] through the weakness of Jesus's death in order "to put to rest" permanently the satanic
adversaries and the archenemy himself.

Truly, through the victory of Jesus's death he was crowned with
glory and honor. Indeed, the cross is the theological center of the universe so that through Christ's redemption, God was "summing up . . .
all things in Christ, things in the heavens and things on the earth" (Eph.
1:10). God "raised Him from the dead and seated Him at His right hand
in the heavenly places. . . . He put all things in subjection under His feet"
(see Eph. 1:20, 22 with Psalm 8:6). At Christ's second coming, "the last
enemy that will be abolished is death." At that time the process begun

at the cross will be completed when God will have "put all things in subjection under His [Jesus's] feet" (1 Cor. 15:26–27 and Ps. 8:6).

Appropriately Martin Luther has remarked in his ageless hymn:

A mighty fortress is our God,
a bulwark never failing; . . .
for still our ancient foe
doth seek to work us woe;
his craft and power are great;
and armed with cruel hate,
on earth is not his equal.

Did we in our own strength confide,
our striving would be losing;
were not the right man on our side,
the man of God's own choosing.
Dost ask who that may be?
Christ Jesus, it is he,
Lord Sabaoth his name,
from age to age the same,
and he must win the battle.

And though this world, with devils filled,
should threaten to undo us,
we will not fear, for God hath willed
his truth to triumph through us.
The prince of darkness grim,
we tremble not for him;
his rage we can endure,
for lo! his doom is sure;
one little word shall fell him. . . .

Let goods and kindred go,
this mortal life also;
the body they may kill:
God's truth abideth still;
his kingdom is forever.

The King Who Had No Crown

The Prince and the Pauper is one of Mark Twain's most beloved short stories. It is about two young boys—Prince Edward, son of King Henry VIII, and an insignificant pauper—both of whom were born on the same day. The pauper boy always dreamed of being a prince, so one day he forced his way into the palace in an attempt to meet and talk with Prince Edward. However, he was immediately apprehended by guards. Prince Edward saw the incident and allowed the pauper to have a private audience with him. Upon hearing that the pauper had always aspired to be a prince, Edward agreed to exchange clothes so the pauper could get a brief glance of what he would look like as a prince. When they had changed clothes, they discovered that they were identical in appearance.

They were then interrupted, and Prince Edward was misjudged as the beggar and thrown out of the palace. As Edward walked through the streets of England, he proclaimed to various passersby that he was the Prince of England, but they only made fun of him. For some time Edward lived a pauper's life. The day came when Henry VIII died, and Edward claimed to crowds on the street that he was king. Again, the people ridiculed him. Although he appeared as a pauper, he really was a king. This was his ironic plight. Edward was finally recognized as king, but only after he had suffered scorn and derision as a pauper.

This fictional story is certainly illustrative of the ironic situation of Christ's life on earth. Although he appeared as a pauper during his earthly ministry, he was really a prince, the messianic king sent by God. As he himself said, "The foxes have holes and the birds of the air have nests, but the Son of Man has nowhere to lay His head" (Matt. 8:20). Psalm 8:4 is one of the first places in the Bible where the phrase "son of man" is associated with the coming Messiah and his kingdom.[16] This subject is developed further in Daniel 7, where the prophet has a vision of the future. Daniel sees that in the end times God will judge the evil world empires (portrayed as fierce animals) and their ultimate ruler, Satan. Their universal kingship will be removed. After this vision Daniel sees this:

> And behold, with the clouds of heaven
> One like a Son of Man was coming,
> And He came up to the Ancient of Days
> And was presented before Him.
> And to Him was given dominion,
> Glory and a kingdom. . . .
> His dominion is an everlasting dominion . . .
> Which will not be destroyed. (Dan. 7:13–14)

Daniel observes that the world dominion removed from the wicked world empires will be transferred to the Son of Man at some point in the distant future. And at this time the Son of Man will be enthroned in glory as world ruler in the presence of God. Daniel's prophecy gave rise to a popular Jewish expectation during the first century AD, that when the Messiah came, he would in some powerful and supernatural way defeat Israel's enemies and reestablish the nation as the dominant world power (see 4 Ezra 12–13; *1 En.* 36–72).[17]

---

16. See also Ps. 80:17–19.

17. See also Psalms of Solomon 17–18. These writings (4 Ezra; 1 Enoch; and Psalms of Solomon) are Jewish writings roughly contemporaneous with the New Testament writings but are not part of the inspired canon of Scripture. Nevertheless, in this case, they give interesting information about messianic expectations.

Intriguingly Jesus's favorite title for himself in the Synoptic Gospels (Matthew, Mark, and Luke) was "Son of Man," which he adopted from Daniel 7:13. The majority of Jews could not accept Jesus as the promised Messiah, the Son of Man, because he did not militarily deliver them from their Roman oppressors as they believed the Son of Man would do. Most Jews could not believe that Jesus was the Son of Man because not only did he not reestablish Israel as a world power, but he died the death of a common criminal.

The fact that Jesus called himself "Son of Man" so often, though he never established a physical kingdom nor wore a king's crown on his head, is especially difficult to understand since Jesus was given opportunity to be crowned as a king but refused (John 6:6–15). Furthermore, Jesus's life during his three-year ministry was characterized primarily by poverty and suffering. The answer to the question of how Jesus could view himself as the royal Son of Man lies in the theme already found in Psalm 8, where the Son of Man was to conquer the satanic forces through apparent weakness and not through physical, military power. The Jews of Jesus's day made the mistake of not identifying the figure of Psalm 8 with that of Daniel 7. The context of Daniel hints that the Son of Man would inherit his kingdom only after a period of suffering. The first indication of this is that believing saints are also said to receive the same eternal kingdom as the Son of Man, but only after they have first suffered:

> That horn [Satan] was waging war with the saints and overpowering them until the Ancient of Days came and judgment was passed in favor of the saints of the Highest One, and the time arrived when the saints took possession of the kingdom. (Dan. 7:21–22; see also 7:18, 24–27)

If the saints must suffer before receiving the same kingdom that the Son of Man will receive, it is likely that he must also suffer before he gains his heavenly throne.[18] That this suggestion is plausible is borne out by Daniel 9:24–27, where the Son of Man from Daniel 7 is referred to as "Messiah the Prince," who "will be cut off and have nothing"; nevertheless, he will make a firm covenant that will make an end of sin, atone for iniquity, and bring in everlasting righteousness.[19]

If the Messiah of Daniel 9 must be cut off and have nothing before he can begin to bring in everlasting righteousness, then the fact that the Son of Man of Daniel 7 must suffer before he can begin to be given an everlasting dominion does not sound odd. Interestingly, Daniel 9 calls the Messiah a prince even though he is "cut off" (killed) and "has nothing," that is, even though he does not have a crown. In some sense he is a prince although he is not yet physically ruling. He even makes a strong ("firm") covenant, ironically through his weakness of being cut off. Probably the Son of Man can also then be considered a royal figure while not ruling in an earthly sense, so that he not merely receives a consummate kingdom after suffering but rules spiritually in the midst of his suffering.

That this is certainly the case is confirmed by Jesus's own understanding of himself as the Son of Man (see Matt. 16:21; Luke 9:22). Although Daniel 7:13 prophetically says that a Son of Man was coming to

---

18. A number of New Testament scholars have made this observation. Interestingly, the climax of the vision in Dan. 7:1–14 is the "son of man" receiving and ruling over an eternal kingdom. One would then expect that the "interpretation" of the vision in Dan. 7:15–26 would highlight the "son of man" explicitly. However, there is no mention of the "son of man" in the interpretive section of Daniel 7. The closest reference to the "son of man" is the repeated reference to the saints receiving and possessing the kingdom forever (Dan. 7:18; so also Dan. 7:22, 27). Since it is unlikely that the interpretive section would not refer in some way to the figure of the "son of man," it is probable that the reference to the "saints receiving the kingdom forever" is intended by Daniel to identify the saints' reception of the kingdom to the son of man's reception of the kingdom in Dan. 7:13–14. This means that the saints are identified with the "son of man" and vice versa. Thus, likewise when the saints are said to suffer before receiving the kingdom, it implies that the "son of man" must suffer before receiving the kingdom.

19. For arguments broadly supporting this interpretation see D. Ford, *Daniel* (Nashville, TN: Southern Publishing Association, 1978).

be enthroned gloriously, Jesus views himself as beginning to fulfill this prophecy through his mission of suffering and dishonor. So Jesus says:

> Whoever wishes to become great among you shall be your servant, and whoever wishes to be first among you shall be your slave; just as the Son of Man did not come to be served, but to serve, and to give His life a ransom for many. (Matt. 20:26–28; Mark 10:45)

Jesus understood his role as the Son of Man from Daniel 7 in light of the Messiah's role in Daniel 9:26–27. So Jesus had come "to give His life a ransom for many." Thus, Jesus refers to himself as the royal Son of Man because he was beginning to reign spiritually—not physically—over the forces of evil. It is true that God had intended that "all the peoples, nations and men of every language might serve" the Son of Man (Dan. 7:14), but for this to occur, Jesus had to serve them by giving his life a ransom for them. This aspect of Jesus's ironic rule is also emphasized in Luke 19:10: "The *Son of Man has come* to seek and to save that which was lost" (cf. Matt. 18:11). Appropriately, Jesus washed the disciples' feet immediately before his being spiritually crowned at the cross, in order to express the serving nature of his mission and saving death (John 13:4–15). He washed their feet to symbolize his role as servant in washing them from their sins.

This ironic kingdom that Jesus was inaugurating has significant practical application for Christians. For example, after Jesus washed the disciples' feet to symbolize his kingly servanthood, he exhorted the disciples to imitate him. The disciples were exhorted to imitate Jesus by washing "one another's feet. For I gave you an example that you should do as I did to you" (John 13:14–15). Jesus was a model. Those who seek their own glory will not be glorified by God, but those who humbly *serve* others will be. Those whom the world glorifies are often not those whom God glorifies. The world honors people on the basis of outward success (whether it be sports stars, movie celebrities, or wealthy persons), but God honors in an ironic manner on the basis of unseen spiritual qualities: "God sees not as man sees, for man looks at the outward appearance, but the Lord looks at the heart" (1 Sam. 16:7).

So it was not different for Jesus, the "author of . . . faith, who for the joy set before Him endured the cross, despising the shame, and has sat down at the right hand of the throne of God" (Heb. 12:2). Paul highlights this ironic idea with respect to both Jesus *and* his followers:

> With humility of mind regard one another as more important than yourselves; do not merely look out for your own personal interests, but also for the interests of others. Have this attitude in yourselves which was also in Christ Jesus, who, although He existed in the form of God, did not regard equality with God a thing to be grasped, but emptied Himself, taking the form of a bond-servant . . . and being found in appearance as a man, He humbled Himself by becoming obedient to the point of death. . . . For this reason also, God highly exalted Him, and bestowed on Him the name which is above every name. (Phil. 2:3–9)

Therefore, "Son of Man" was Jesus's favorite title to designate the ironic character of his royal pre-crucifixion ministry in which he gave up the use of his divine attributes and assumed an inglorious lifestyle of suffering and humble servanthood. He viewed himself as beginning to fulfill the Daniel 7:13 enthronement prophecy ironically through his ministry of suffering and weakness; what appeared to Daniel in prophetic vision as a Son of Man, gloriously proceeding before God's throne to receive heavenly rule, begins fulfillment on earth as an enigmatic, inglorious, three-year procession climaxed at Jesus's reception of kingship before the divine throne at the ascension (see diagram below). And the Son of Man's royal court was composed of "tax collectors and sinners" (Luke 7:34). Indeed, the kingdom he was establishing was invisible to the naked eye, as he said: "The kingdom of God is not coming with signs to be observed; nor will they say, 'Look, here it is!' or, 'There it is!' For behold, the kingdom of God is in your midst" (Luke 17:20–21). As a consequence, for Jesus, Daniel 7 and Psalm 8 concerned the same messianic prophecy, that the Son of Man would defeat evil through apparent weakness.

At his second coming Christ will complete his mission as Son of Man, when he will judge evil and vindicate the righteous (cf. Mark 13:24–27; 14:62). Then the Daniel 7 prophecy will also be fulfilled in the earthly, material realm.

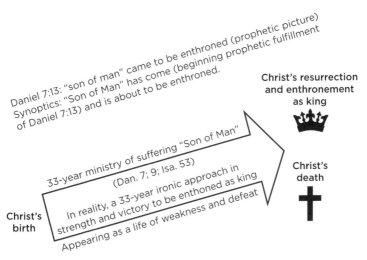

Although the approach to enthronement in Daniel 7:13 seems quite brief, Christ sees it as referring to his 33-year ministry on earth leading to his enthronement at the resurrection.

The Serpent and the Son

According to ancient Greek mythology Asclepius was the god of healing. In times of illness the Greeks would turn in prayer to this god to request a cure. He was the physician god and was referred to as "savior" because he saved men's bodies from disease and death. The worship of Asclepius became a religion in itself, and temples were erected for religious practice. The most predominant symbol of this god was a serpent, which was supposedly his earthly incarnation. Indeed, serpent images were placed in all the temples to represent Asclepius. Sometimes he was symbolized as a bearded man holding a rod with a serpent coiled around it. It was believed that the serpent regularly helped in curing the suffering petitioner.

One of the central rituals of the Asclepian worship service was known as "the taking up of the rod" (with the serpent on it). This "lifting" ritual was meant to indicate that Asclepius was in the process of performing a healing for someone. Presumably, this healing could occur only through the faith of the worshiper. Scholars have inquired about why the serpent represented Asclepius and why it symbolized the power of healing, but no satisfactory answers have been found. Nevertheless, the ritual of "taking up the rod" with a serpent has intriguing parallels with one of Christ's important sayings in the New Testament.

In the previous section concerning the Son of Man, we saw how Jesus understood himself as fulfilling Daniel's Son of Man prophecy by ironically ruling through the suffering and apparent defeat at the cross. In John's Gospel there is a "Son of Man" saying that deserves further notice, since it sheds even more light on Jesus's ironic mission at his first coming. In John 3:14–15 Jesus makes a very enigmatic comparison about his role as Son of Man, which is strikingly similar to the Greek picture of the rod and serpent being lifted up in Asclepian worship:

> As Moses lifted up the serpent in the wilderness, even so must the Son of Man be lifted up; so that whoever believes will in Him have eternal life.

Although the origin and explanation of the lifting up of the serpent image in ancient Greek religion remains a mystery, the reason for Jesus's reference to the same image *is* clear. Therefore, why does Jesus compare himself to a serpent, perhaps even a symbol for Satan?[20] In order to answer, we must realize that Jesus is referring to an episode that happened to Israel in their wilderness wanderings after they had been delivered from Egypt. Throughout their wanderings Israel continuously murmured against the Lord whenever need arose. At one point Israel grumbled because they had no food, so God graciously provided manna for them. However, they did not see such provision as good enough. Numbers 21:5 records Israel saying, "We loath this miserable food [manna]." As a result, "the LORD sent fiery serpents among the people and they bit the people, so that many people of Israel died" (v. 6). The people then confessed their sin and asked Moses to pray to the Lord that he would remove this judgment from them (v. 7). Again, God compassionately responded to their request:

> Then the LORD said to Moses, "Make a fiery serpent, and set it on a standard; and it shall come about, that everyone who is bitten, when he looks at it, he will live." And Moses made a bronze serpent and set it on the standard; and it came about, that if a serpent bit any man, when he looked to the bronze serpent, he lived. (Num. 21:8–9)

---

20. At least half of the uses of the word *serpent* in the New Testament refer to Satan, as may also more subtly be the case in the Old Testament.

God had judged Israel's sin by cursing them with death, which was brought about by serpents sent by the Lord to attack the Israelites with lethal poisonous bites. Yet God again graciously listened to Moses's request and provided a way of escape. Moses was commanded to make a bronze copy of the lethal serpents and to place it on a pole. Then all who had been bitten were to look upon the bronze serpent, and they would be enabled to live. No doubt, the victims were to look to the bronze serpent in faith as God's provision to save them physically. The odd thing about this divine provision of healing was that the object of faith in which the bitten sufferer was to trust was a model of the very thing that had caused his suffering. The very thing causing their death—a serpent—they were to believe in so that they could be given their life.

Why did God design such an *ironic sign* of healing in the Old Testament episode? Interestingly, the Hebrew (and Greek) word for "standard" (or "pole") upon which the serpent was to be placed can also mean "sign." Apparently God intended this sign in order to show that he was sovereignly able to reverse the curses by transforming them into blessings. The bronze serpent lifted up by Moses demonstrated that the curse of the deadly serpent bites could be turned into a blessing of life for those who believed. This intention could be similar to that in Genesis 3 where Adam's wife is named Eve, meaning "life," a name, as we have seen, that is related to a word meaning "serpent." In both passages the death brought by the serpents is turned into life, and in both there are *signs* (respectively, a name and an image) symbolically to designate the ironic reversal.

This idea of having faith in the curse of death in order to obtain the blessing of life explains and solves the mystery of why Jesus compares himself with a serpent in John 3:14: Jesus sees that the Son of Man being lifted up on the cross is a death curse in which spiritually dying men need to trust so that the blessing of eternal life may come, "that whoever believes in Him may have eternal life." We trust in Christ's curse of death to obtain eternal life in that Christ suffered as a substitute on the cross for sinful man by undergoing the eternal penalty of spiritual death that man deserved. "For God . . . gave His only begotten Son, that whoever believes in Him shall not perish, but have eternal life. For God did not send the Son into the world to judge the world, but that the world might be saved through Him" (John 3:16–17).

Christ lifts away the sin of the world (John 1:29) by being lifted up on the cross. When a person trusts in God's provision, he is delivered from eternal death to life, which begins at the moment of belief. As was true with the Israelites in regard to the bronze serpent, so today if one doesn't look in faith to the death sign of the cross, that person will be cursed with spiritual death. If a person does not believe that Christ has taken the eternal penalty of sin, then that person must suffer it. When people refuse God's provision to heal them from the deadly bite of the satanic serpent, then God has no other choice but to allow them to perish forever.

In John 3:14 it is also evident that Christ saw Moses's lifting up of the bronze serpent as a *typological prophecy* of his own lifting up upon the cross. Notice that he says, "As Moses lifted up the serpent in the wilderness, even so *must* [or "it is necessary for"] the Son of Man [to] be lifted up." This was an event that by its very nature pointed forward and as such necessitated its fulfillment in the cross. God's predictions must always be fulfilled.

Finally, verse 14 also appears to be a double entendre. That is, the phrase "be lifted up" has a *double meaning*. First, it refers to Jesus being literally lifted up in death on the cross, which is clear from the parallel with the symbolic curse of the serpent that Moses lifted up. Furthermore, Jesus uses the same phrase, "lifted up," in John 12:32 clearly to refer to his death. John even comments in 12:33 that "He was saying this to indicate the kind of death by which he was to die." Second, however, Jesus's being lifted up is also an allusion to his resurrection, which is intimated by Jesus's statement at the end of 12:32, that he would "draw all men to [himself]." John 3:13 refers to the Son of Man's ascension, where also it relates directly to his being lifted up in verse 14. As well, verse 15 asserts that belief in Jesus's "lifting up" results in life. In John 12:32 the phrase appears as a further explanation of Jesus's teaching about resurrection life:

> "And I, if I am lifted up from the earth, will draw all men to Myself." . . . He was saying this to indicate the kind of death by which he should die. (12:32–33)

Therefore, Jesus's lifting up refers to two apparently opposite things: (1) his *death* on the cross and (2) his *resurrection* to life. However, the apparent antithetical meaning is intended to show that Christ's judgment of death on the cross was to be changed into his deliverance at the resurrection. His lifting up at the cross was but a necessary prelude to his being lifted up in resurrection. This juxtaposition beautifully reveals the unity of Christ's work of salvation. He had to die on the cross as a vicarious sacrifice for man's sin, but if he had not been resurrected, he would have remained under sin's death penalty—and all mankind with him. Yet, the resurrection was his victory over sin's penalty and the victory of all those who trust Christ as their penal substitute. Hence, Christ's death and resurrection are two inseparable sides of the same coin of salvation. Jesus's death ironically was as much of a victory as his resurrection. But there is more. It is not only Jesus's lifting up in resurrection that draws all men to him, but also his very lifting up on the cross. That means that in his very death, even before the overt victory of the resurrection, Jesus's dying was a victorious redemptive-historical act that would draw people to him, which would benefit people redemptively. Thus, the death in and of itself, even before the resurrection, was an ironic expression of strength and victory.

The Hanging Tree

Galatians 3:13–14 has already been mentioned briefly, but more ought to be said about how it contributes to the ironic theme of God creating the blessing of salvation out of the cursing of final judgment, especially as this irony relates to Jesus's work at the cross. Paul claims that Christ saved believers "from the *curse* of the Law, having become a *curse* for us." To prove that Jesus took humanity's eternal curse at the cross, Paul quotes from Deuteronomy 21:23: "For it is written, 'Cursed is everyone who hangs on a tree.'" The apostle concludes that Jesus was cursed on the "tree" [or "cross"] "in order that . . . the blessing of Abraham [i.e., of salvation] might come."

But why does Paul quote from Deuteronomy, and what does the quotation mean? To answer, we look at Deuteronomy 21:22: "If a man has committed a sin worthy of death . . . he is [to be] put to death, and you hang him on a tree." Some first-century Jews understood this passage to be applicable to crucifixion, which was a natural application since the Greek word (in the Greek Old Testament[21]) for tree (*xulon*) in Deuteronomy 21 can be translated as "cross" in the New Testament. But, again, it must be asked, why would Paul apply to Christ a passage associated with one of the worst Old Testament criminal punishments? Those in Israel who committed sins "worthy of death," such as murder, homosexuality, blasphemy, and rape, were not only to be stoned to death but subsequently hung on a tree until sundown in order to demonstrate the shame and disgrace of the crime. Such a person was the most accursed of God in the

---

21. The Old Testament was originally written in Hebrew, and centuries later, before the New Testament period, it was translated into Greek.

whole nation. Most Jews would have identified Jesus as deserving this cursed death because he blasphemed by ascribing to himself the title of Messiah and the divine Son of God. And such an accursed one could not possibly have been the true Son of God, they thought, since God would never allow his true Son to unjustly undergo such a cursed, shameful punishment of hanging on a tree. Such a punishment was reserved for the most heinous of criminals.

This is probably the main reason that the Jews rejected Jesus's messianic and divine claims. How could the most blessed and glorious person of Israel—the coming Messiah—be at the same time the most cursed and abominable? Therefore, a faithful Jew daring to confess such a despised being as God's Messiah would have been blasphemous. And for the zealously religious Jew, like Paul, there was even the desire to persecute those Jews who were so confessing this despicable Jesus as their Messiah. Truly, Messiah crucified was to the Jews a "stumbling block" (1 Cor. 1:23).

Because of our previous discussion, the answer to this Jewish dilemma is readily at hand, and it is reiterated by Paul in Galatians 3:13–14. The Messiah *had to suffer the eternal curse of God* that his people (composed of Jews and Gentiles) deserved for their rebellious sin of breaking his moral law (cf. Gal. 3:10–12), which made them heinous criminals in God's eyes. Therefore, what many Jews thought was blasphemous—to confess Jesus crucified as their Messiah and Savior—was, in reality, the most righteous thing they could have done, since this was the very way to salvation. The curse from Deuteronomy is viewed by Paul as the ultimate means by which people can be blessed with salvation.[22] The dishonor of *hanging* in this Old Testament passage is viewed as an ironic foreshadowing of the *hanging* of Christ, which led to his honor. "For the wages of

---

22. For some of the background of this discussion on Deuteronomy see Seyoon Kim, *The Origin of Paul's Gospel* (Grand Rapids, MI: Eerdmans, 1982), 46–50, 287.

sin is death, but the free gift of God is eternal life in Christ Jesus our Lord" (Rom. 6:23). He was hanged so that we might not have to be. Jesus's damnation at the cross accomplishes our salvation, *if we believe* he died for us.

A Misunderstanding of God's Law?

Galatians 3 explains that the curse that Christ bore for humanity was the curse that humanity deserved for breaking God's law. Many people today do not understand exactly why it was necessary that Christ had to bear this eternal curse for humanity's violation of the law. Why is there this lack of understanding? The answer can be found by exploring the background of how so many in our culture conceive of divine law.

People often think of God's law in Scripture as the Ten Commandments. Of course, many more laws beside these were given to Israel, but all the various laws delivered to the nation were expressions or applications in one form or another of the Ten Commandments. Although most in Western society do not know each of the Ten Commandments, they have a general idea of some, usually those among the last five (i.e., the commandments against dishonoring parents, murder, adultery, stealing, bearing false witness, and coveting). Whatever accurate knowledge people have of God's moral law in Scripture, there seems to be a general misunderstanding of its purpose. If asked, most would probably say that the purpose of God's law is that people might be saved by becoming righteous through obeying it.

Of course, no one would claim that anyone could perfectly obey God's law, since no one expects God to demand perfection as a requirement to enter heaven after death. It is typically thought that if one's life is characterized more by obedience than disobedience, then the scales of divine justice will tilt in a favorable direction pointing to salvation. This concept is not new. It was held by many Jews during the time of Jesus,[23] and it has been held by many professing Christians throughout church history.[24] "Salvation by works" is the label some have given to this doctrine. However, this is a misunderstanding that lies at the heart of humanity's inability to perceive the necessity of why Christ had to bear humanity's curse. On the contrary, one can find a beginning explanation of the real intent of the law in Galatians 3:10–11:

> For as many as are of the works of the Law are under a curse; for it is written, "Cursed is everyone who does not abide by all things written in the book of the Law, to perform them." Now that no one is justified [declared righteous] by the Law before God is evident.

Paul's point is tersely summarized in Galatians 5:3: "I testify again to every man who receives circumcision, that he is under obligation to keep the whole Law." In other words, those who attempt to achieve salvation through good works by obeying God's laws are doomed to fail because God *does* expect perfection, and therefore nothing imperfect or unholy can enter into the holy presence of God. The futility of trying to save oneself through obedience to the law is expressed well by James, who explains that you could perfectly obey all your life and yet disobey only once, and that is enough to make you as guilty as if you had broken the whole law (see James 2:10). In other words, even *one* violation can keep you from the saving presence of God.

What then can the purpose of the law be, if God did not give it to us in order that we might obey it to obtain salvation? The apostle Paul asked the same question: "Why the Law then? It was added be-

---

23. On which, e.g., cf. J. Piper, *The Justification of God: An Exegetical and Theological Study of Romans 9:1–23* (Grand Rapids, MI: Baker, 1983), 132–35.

24. Pelagius of the fifth century AD is one of the earliest and best representatives of this view.

cause of transgressions" (Gal. 3:19). Paul means that the main intention of God's law was to demonstrate to humans how sinful they are. Paul says of himself elsewhere, "I would not have come to know sin except through the Law; for I would not have known about coveting if the Law had not said, 'You shall not covet'" (Rom. 7:7). Without the law, humanity would not only not know what is right but would have no knowledge of sin. The law has *a condemning purpose* in that it shows people how sinful they really are and how far short they fall from attaining salvation through obedience. The ultimate aim of the law is perhaps best stated in Romans 3:19–20, 23:

> Now we know that whatever the Law says, it speaks to those who are under the Law, so that every mouth may be closed and all the world may become accountable to God; because by the works of the Law no flesh will be justified [declared righteous] in His sight; for through the Law comes the knowledge of sin. . . . For all have sinned and fall short of the glory of God.

Consequently, the law has the purpose of revealing to humanity their sin and showing them that they deserve condemnation for their sin. Humans cannot perfectly obey the law because they have a sin nature, and the law acts as an irritant, arousing in people a desire to break it (see Rom. 7:8–13). Accordingly, the aim of God's commandments for sinful people was never to impart life or salvation but, ironically, *the very opposite*—to disclose an awareness of sin and its accompanying death or judgment. Mankind has ironically turned things around (Isa. 29:16) by believing that obedience to the law can lead to eternal life, when it really directs one only in a reverse direction, to eternal death. Possibly the unbelieving situation Paul had found himself in is generally applicable to mankind: "The good that I want, I do not do, but I practice the very evil that I do not want" (Rom. 7:19).[25] Unbelieving people have this contradiction within their own being.

So the law was not "given . . . to impart life" but to "shut up everyone under sin. . . . Therefore the Law has become our tutor to lead us to Christ, that we may be justified by faith," and not by obedience to the law (Gal. 3:21–24). The law is intended to make people realize their sin and the coming curse on account of it, and also to teach them to look to Christ who can "redeem [them] from the curse of the Law, having become a curse for [them]" in order that they may gain salvation (Gal. 3:13–14). For "now apart from the Law the righteousness of God [which man needs] has been manifested . . . through faith in Jesus Christ for all those who believe" (Rom. 3:21–22). Hence, although the apparent life-giving law of God imposes eternal death upon us, the sacrificial death of Jesus can turn our death into eternal life. Thus, the condemning purpose of the law was ultimately reversed ironically by the God-man who *perfectly* obeyed it and, at the same time, suffered our penalty for breaking it. As a result, we are enabled to gain his perfection by faith and enter into God's holy and saving presence.[26]

---

25. It is debated whether Rom. 7:8–25 refers to a conflict within the believer or within the unbeliever. Though many commentators prefer the former, I see it to be more likely that here Paul is speaking of the latter, especially of the conflict that characterized Paul's life before he came to faith (on which see G. K. Beale, *A New Testament Biblical Theology* [Grand Rapids, MI: Baker, 2011], 845–47).

26. The additional purposes of the law are: (1) to restrain sin in the civil realm by threatening judgments for the breaking of God's moral laws, and (2) to enlighten Christians to know what to delight in and how to please God. For a somewhat different view of the law in Galatians, see T. D. Gordon, *Promise, Law, Faith: Covenant-Historical Reasoning in Galatians* (Peabody, MA: Hendrickson, 2019), who contends that "law" in Galatians consistently refers to the Sinai covenant that God made with Israel.

4

The Christian Life:

Power Is Perfected in the Powerless

The wounded surgeon plies the steel that questions the distempered part; Beneath the bleeding hands we feel the sharp compassion of the healer's art. . . . Who then devised the torment? Love.

—T. S. Eliot, *Four Quartets*, "East Coker IV"

How often do the youngest get picked on by their older brothers and get the raw end of the deal? The Old Testament story of Joseph illustrates this more than most modern examples could. But what happened to Joseph is, above all, an Old Testament picture of the truth encapsulated in Romans 8:28, that "God causes all things to work together for good to those who love God." It is an event reflecting the principle of how God ironically causes a good turnabout in all the ill fortunes of the godly.

Joseph's brothers despised him. Their hatred stemmed from their jealousy that their father loved Joseph more than them. Also, Joseph told his brothers that it had been revealed to him that he would rule over them in the future, despite his lower standing in the family. Consequently, Joseph's brothers vented their vengeful and jealous anger by selling him as a slave to an Arab camel caravan carrying trading goods to Egypt. In Egypt he was then sold as a servant in Potiphar's household, the captain of Pharaoh's bodyguard (see Gen. 37). Joseph distinguished himself in Potiphar's eyes and was rewarded with promotion to the highest position in the household, managing all of his master's affairs. However, when Potiphar's wife tried to seduce Joseph and he refused, she angrily accused him of trying to seduce her. As a result, Joseph was sent to jail. But, again, Joseph distinguished himself according to God's grace, and he was put in charge over all the affairs of the prison (Gen. 39). During this time Joseph also demonstrated a unique skill of interpreting prophetic dreams of fellow prisoners (Gen. 41). His circumstances notwithstanding, he continued to believe that God had good purposes to bring out of his bad situation. During his imprisonment, the word of the Lord refined Joseph that he might teach others wisdom (Ps. 105:19, 22). Thus God used Joseph's circumstances to cause him to trust God more and to be increasingly sanctified.

A time came when Pharaoh had a dream in which he saw seven healthy cows devoured by seven unhealthy cows, and he had another dream in which he saw seven full ears of grain on a stalk followed by seven thin ears of grain. In both dreams, that which was unhealthy and thin swallowed up the healthy and full. After finding no one who could decipher the dreams, the king heard about a Hebrew named Joseph who had an uncanny ability to interpret symbolic dreams. He sent for Joseph, and the skillful Hebrew accurately unfolded the dream's meaning. Joseph explained that the dream was a prophecy from God of Egypt's future: Egypt would experience seven years of abundance followed by seven years of famine. Joseph also proposed a solution to the coming famine.

After discerning Joseph's prophetic ability and administrative wisdom, Pharaoh made him second in authority over all of Egypt. In essence, Joseph ruled Egypt for Pharaoh (Gen. 41), and Joseph finally saw how God had caused good to emerge from his former evil circumstances.

When famine struck, people from surrounding areas seeking aid converged on Egypt, since Egypt was prepared for the food shortage. Among those coming for help were Joseph's brothers. To summarize this vivid story, we find the brothers approaching Joseph's throne to request food for their families back in Canaan. After a time, Joseph dramatically reveals his identity to his brothers:

> Then Joseph could not control himself before all those who stood by him, and he cried. . . . Then Joseph said to his brothers, "Please come closer to me." . . . And he said, "I am your brother Joseph, whom you sold into Egypt. Now do not be grieved or angry with yourselves, because you sold me here, for God sent me before you to preserve [your] life. For the famine has been in the land these two years. . . . God sent me before you to preserve for you a remnant in the earth, and to keep you alive by a great deliverance." (Gen. 45:1, 4–7)

Following his disclosure, Joseph's brothers and their families came to live in Egypt and remained there until Israel's exodus from that land a few generations later.

Joseph's startling revelation to his brothers upon their reunion demonstrates that he perceived God's purpose in the previous events. Out of jealousy the brothers had tried to ruin Joseph's life by selling him into slavery to a place of apparent no return. But Joseph now realized God had a purpose in all this. Through Joseph's terrible bondage in slavery, God was planning to prosper him and his family so that ultimately Joseph was able to say, "God sent me before you to preserve for you a remnant." At a later point, when his brothers again became fearful that Joseph might want revenge for their wicked deed, he responded similarly:

> Do not be afraid, for am I in God's place? As for you, you meant evil against me, but God meant it for good in order to bring about this present result, to preserve many people alive. (Gen. 50:19–20)

Out of Joseph's brothers' evil plans, God had brought about good. Human plans can never thwart God's but only fulfill the ultimate divine intention. Interestingly, God had arranged that Joseph and then the rest of his family would settle in Egypt because Joseph's brothers were becoming too much a part of Canaanite pagan culture. If God had allowed this melting-pot process to continue, the very national identity of Israel as a set-apart instrument of the Lord would have been compromised and with it God's intention to bless "all the families of the earth" through Israel (see Gen. 12:3). Therefore, God set in motion a series of events, primarily the famine, that would first propel the families of Israel into Egypt and would then take care of them once they were there. God had planned Egypt to be the womb in which these families would grow until he gave birth to them at the exodus as the formal nation of Israel, God's firstborn son (see Ex. 4:22).[1]

This story is a classic example of the principle by which God sovereignly oversees the lives of his saints by causing "all things to work

---

1. This birth metaphor of Egypt and the exodus is taken from a lecture by B. K. Waltke, "Old Testament Introduction," at Dallas Theological Seminary (Fall 1972).

together for good to those who love God" (Rom. 8:28). He reverses the adversity of the faithful and ironically restores their prosperity. The very tortuous route Joseph took to the prison house in Egypt was simultaneously the very road to his pleasurable rule in the pharaoh's house. Joseph in a sense was delivered to Egypt, and this led to Joseph's brothers becoming "a remnant in the earth," going to Egypt from a lethal famine and the temptations of pagan influence (Gen. 45:7).

Joseph's life contains a pattern inherent in the lives of all Christians. We can identify with bad turns of events, especially those times in which we are mistreated by others as was Joseph. Yet God blessed Joseph and promoted him in Potiphar's household so that he began to overcome the injury dealt him by his brothers. But while he was surmounting his unfortunate circumstances, Joseph was inflicted with another setback through Potiphar's wife, and he went to prison. Many of us can identify with this. We suffer something undeservedly, then over time we begin to overcome it, but before we fully do, we undergo another setback. Nevertheless, we should not lose heart. Joseph didn't. He continued to trust God, and indeed God again turned his cursed situation into a blessed one. Joseph was transformed from a prisoner of his brothers and of the Egyptians to a ruler over prisoners, and finally into the ruler of Egypt.

Truly, "God causes all things to work together for good to those who love God" (Rom. 8:28). We often observe Christians who appear to trust God for their lives when everything is going well. But Joseph's life and Romans 8 instruct us that it is especially when we are in the "pits" (see Gen. 37:20–28)—when we are suffering setbacks—that we are to trust the Lord's sovereign guidance of our lives. In fact, God places us in such situations so that we may believe that he will reverse them for our good and his glory! When we are at the lowest point in our Christian life, we need to remember that "in all these things we overwhelmingly *conquer* through Him" (Rom. 8:37). If he doesn't do it in this life, as he did with Joseph and Job, he will do so for us ultimately in the next life, as he did with Jesus, Peter, and Paul.

The ironic situation of the Christian life is meant to induce faith in us; indeed, it demands faith from us! As was the case with Joseph, so with Christians: "Many who are . . . last [will be] first" (Matt. 19:30), and "whoever wishes to become great among you shall be your servant; and whoever wishes to be first among you shall be slave of all" (Mark 10:43–44). It was only when Joseph lost what he thought was to be his life that he truly found his life, for "he who has lost his life for my sake shall find it" (Matt. 10:39; 25). Hence, the evil of Joseph's bondage was ironically meant to bring about good.

Bringing Good Out of Evil

The life of the Christian is based on and modeled after that of Jesus Christ. Christ persevered in his faith in spite of pressures to compromise and was killed because of it. Nevertheless, his death was reversed into life and was overcome through resurrection. Jesus's ironic overcoming is pictured in Revelation 5:5–6, 11–12:

> Behold, the Lion that is from the tribe of Judah. . . . And I saw . . . a Lamb standing, as if slain. . . . And I heard the voice of many angels . . . saying with a loud voice, "Worthy is the Lamb that was slain to receive power and riches and wisdom and might and honor and glory and blessing."

Jesus conquered the forces of evil through both his death and his resurrection. John first hears that Jesus overcame as a lion (Rev. 5:5), but when he sees a vision of his Lord, he perceives exactly in what manner Jesus won his victory: Jesus overcame by being overcome at the cross. The cross itself was an invisible victory over satanic forces and was subsequently expressed visibly in his resurrection body. So the Lamb slew his spiritual opponents by allowing himself to be slain temporarily (see Rev. 1:18; cf. 4:67 and 5:5–6 with 15:21). This is why immediately before his death he told his disciples, "Take courage; I have *overcome* the world" (John 16:33).

Christians should reflect in their lives the same paradoxical pattern of their Lord's life. We also must persevere in faith through temptations to compromise. When we remain steadfast in belief, we also, like our Savior, will suffer tribulation. Yet our victory lies in the continued maintenance of faith in the face of discouraging circumstances. Jesus says, "If any one wishes to come after me, he must deny himself, and take up his cross and follow Me" (Matt. 16:24). Christ is saying not merely that we should model our lives after his life but that it must be so modeled, and will be, if we are genuine believers. Christians must overcome through faith while suffering, as Jesus did.

I have tried to show how Romans 8:28 relates to the Joseph account. It is also helpful to focus on this verse in its immediate context in Romans 8. Just as God did for his Son, so for his adopted sons he is always at work turning bad situations ultimately (whether in this life or later) into good ones, reversing defeat into victory. This general principle of ironic reversion, according to which God is constantly working in favor of his people, is set forth lucidly in this twenty-eighth verse: "And we know that *God causes all things* to work together for good to those who love God," those who have trusted in Christ's saving death (see also vv. 30–34). Roman Christians to whom Paul was writing needed to be reminded of this truth since they were undergoing various forms of suffering and persecution because of their faith. Just as we today might be tempted to feel forsaken by God, so Paul's original readers were fearful that their lamentable circumstances could be an indication that God had abandoned and forgotten them. Beleaguered Christians at Rome apparently were unaware that nothing could *separate* them from the love of Christ, whether "tribulation, or distress, or persecution, or famine, or nakedness, or peril, or sword" (Rom. 8:35).

God is unswervingly active in bringing about good from troublesome circumstances in the Christian's life, whether persecution, illness, sin, and all those things that affect us in a fallen world. Although at times it may not be apparent that God is acting for our welfare, such is truly the case. We need to believe in God's promise and not merely in external factors. Since God has shown that he is for us because he "did not spare His own Son, but delivered Him over for us all," nothing in the created order "will be able to separate us from the love of God, which is in Christ Jesus our Lord" (Rom. 8:32, 39).

Paul's principle has been illustrated in Armando Valladares's account of his experiences in a Cuban prison. Valladares suffered an unjust twenty-two-year prison sentence in Communist Cuba. He said after his release:

> Political prisoners were executed by firing squads. . . . Night after night the firing was punctuated with cries of 'Long live Christ the King!' . . . from prisoners as they went to their deaths. . . . I was taken to Boniato prison. . . . All the doors and windows were steel-shuttered. That period was one of the worst. But I felt myself neither alone nor abandoned because God was with me inside that jail. The greater the hatred my jailors directed at me, the more my heart brimmed over with Christian love and faith.[2]

However, while God gave Valladares spiritual victory in the midst of physical suffering, he also caused Valladares's horrible imprison-

---

2. See Armando Valladares, "Inside Castro's Prisons," *Time*, August 15, 1983, 20.

ment to work together for good through his subsequent release to the free world.

Paul compares Christians undergoing adversity to slaughtered sheep: "For Your sake . . . we were considered as sheep to be slaughtered" (Rom. 8:36). Not that every Christian dies for the faith, but "slain sheep" becomes a symbol of the woes that believers endure in their life of faith. Nonetheless, surely "in all these things we overwhelmingly conquer [or overcome] through Him [Christ] who loved us" (Rom. 8:37). Paul is recalling to his readers' minds that their lives must follow the same ironic path of their Savior, who won a victory in the midst of dying. Christ's followers can overcome in no other way than that which Jesus did—through being faithful in the midst of defeat or suffering, even up to the point of death. The apostle John aptly summarizes this idea:

> For whatever is born of God *overcomes* the world; and this is the *victory* that has *overcome* the world—our faith. Who is the one who overcomes the world, but he who believes that Jesus is the Son of God? (1 John 5:4–5)

For such people "God causes all things to work together for good."

The Surpassing Greatness of the Power of Weakness

Biblical principles such as overcoming through being overcome and becoming great by first being a servant are only two of the ways in which the New Testament speaks about the ironic Christian life. In 2 Corinthians 4:7–11 Paul explains how "the surpassing greatness of the power . . . of God" (v. 7) is expressed in the life of the believer:

> We are afflicted in every way, but not crushed; perplexed, but not despairing; persecuted, but not forsaken; struck down, but not destroyed; always carrying about in the body the

dying of Jesus, so that the life of Jesus also may be manifested in our body. For we who live are constantly being delivered over to death for Jesus' sake, so that the life of Jesus also may be manifested in our mortal flesh.

Again, we find the repeated idea that Christian defeat and suffering is an imitation of Christ's and that the Christian's ultimate destiny is also patterned after that of Jesus: God will turn their defeat into victory and their suffering into the joy of triumph, if they continue in faith (vv. 16–18).

The Christian life is truly a paradoxical one:

> In everything [we commend] ourselves as servants of God . . . by glory and dishonor, by evil report and good report; regarded as deceivers and yet true; as unknown yet well-known [to God], as dying yet behold, we live; as punished yet not put to death, as sorrowful yet always rejoicing, as poor yet making many rich, as having nothing yet possessing all things. (2 Cor. 6:4–10)

Paul's words are probably a comprehensive description of a believer's life. Unbelievers, affected by worldly values, view Christians superficially in one way, while God sees them in a diametrically opposite way, as they truly are.

There was a gardener who worked at a university I attended. In contrast to the famous theologians there, he had no education to speak of and was apparently not noticed by the well-known professors and students passing by on the way to classes. But this gardener knew his Bible and tried to apply its truths to his life. He had a vital personal relationship with Jesus Christ and was a man of prayer. Although he could not read his Bible in Greek and Hebrew like the academic theologians, he knew the heart of its message in English and lived according to it. He had written no books nor accumulated any degrees, and his speech sounded uneducated. To the world he was unknown, but to God, well-known. He was poor but spiritually rich (see Rev. 2:9) and appeared "as having nothing yet possessing all things" (2 Cor. 6:10). He was likely regarded by theological scholars as ignorant and *deceived* because he actually believed the Bible was God's word and that Jesus was really God, yet it was he who possessed *true* belief. And some of the professors who were well known for their scholarly writings were actually deceivers, unknown and poor in God's sight, for in their worldly wisdom they had come to disbelieve many of the crucial truths of Scripture.

Foolishness Is Wisdom?

How many in the world think that the gospel is foolishness and that they are too intellectual to believe such an outmoded fable about God, that he became man and died as a substitute for human sin and rose bodily from the grave? Some years ago a book was written by a group of theologians entitled *The Myth of God Incarnate*.[3] The book argues that Jesus himself never claimed to be God—in fact was not God—but that later generations of Christians came to believe this legend or myth about him. But it is not merely modern theologians who espouse such views. Indeed, a significant percentage of our society views the gospel as intellectual foolishness. It may satisfy children or peasants but not them.

But Paul described first-century attitudes in similar terms when he said that many "became futile in their speculations, and their foolish heart was darkened. Professing to be wise, they became fools" (Rom. 1:21–22). However, the true believer must become foolish in the eyes of the world in order to become truly wise. For many

---

3. John Hick, ed., *The Myth of God Incarnate* (Philadelphia: Westminster, 1977).

"search for wisdom; but we preach Christ crucified . . . to Gentiles foolishness, but . . . Christ [is] . . . the wisdom of God. Because the foolishness of God is wiser than men" (1 Cor. 1:22–25). The Jews could not bring themselves to believe that the crucified Jesus was Messiah because they expected the Messiah to be the most honored person in Israel's history. For different reasons Greeks could not trust in Jesus because they didn't believe in the supernatural: "Now when they heard of the resurrection of the dead [i.e., Jesus's resurrection], some began to sneer" (Acts 17:32), "for the word of the cross is foolishness to those who are perishing" (1 Cor. 1:18).

I became a Christian as a freshman in college. Soon afterward I began taking courses in religion because I was excited at the prospect of being able to study Scripture in an academic environment. However, it became apparent immediately that the professors teaching the courses did not believe in the historic doctrines of biblical faith. Rather, they expressed skepticism at anything miraculous recorded in the Bible. I would occasionally speak up in class in an attempt to answer the professor's criticisms, but my responses were met only by witty remarks that side-stepped the essential issue at hand. I was seen by some professors as quite naive for believing in the historicity of such things as Adam's fall, Noah's flood, and Jesus's bodily resurrection. But, as we have seen, what the world views as wise is foolish and vice versa. The values of this world are reversed:

> Let no man deceive himself. If any man among you thinks that he is wise in this age, he must become foolish, so that he may become wise. (1 Cor. 3:18)

Christians are to be "fools for Christ's sake" (1 Cor. 4:10) and endure the ridicule when it comes, as it will.

Where Can I Find Strength to Go On?

Many Christians find themselves in depressing situations and feel they have no more strength to go on in life. Some experience the long, drawn-out suffering and death of a loved one. Others experience financial disasters, emotionally wrenching family problems, and a host of other disappointments, failures, and setbacks. Every Christian at one time or other will ask, "How can I go on?"

Even Jesus himself said, concerning his impending death at the cross, "My Father, if it is possible, let this cup [of suffering] pass from Me" (Matt. 26:39). And yet Jesus's death was the beginning climax (together with his resurrection) of everything he accomplished in his earthly ministry. In the greatest apparent weakness of death, Jesus ironically found his greatest strength in defeating Satan, sin, and death and saving his people.

Our experience can be no different from our Lord's. We also find our greatest strength in what seems to be profound weakness. Paul had this in mind when he said that the weakness of God is stronger than men and that God has chosen the weak things of the world to shame the strong (1 Cor. 1:25, 27). Confidence in fleshly strength accomplishes nothing for God, but he chooses to use Christians for his service when they appear to be at their weakest. "'Not by might nor by power [of the flesh], but by My spirit,' says the LORD of hosts" (Zech. 4:6). When Israel had become militarily weak, and the major world power of the time, Assyria, was about to conquer them, Israel's King Hezekiah affirmed his faith in God's power, saying, "Do not fear . . . because of the king of Assyria . . . for the one with us is greater than the one with him. With him is only an arm of flesh, but with us is the LORD" (2 Chron. 32:7–8). Israel was not defeated, because "the LORD sent an angel who destroyed every mighty warrior" of the Assyrian army (32:21).

The weapons of the Christian's warfare are no different from those of Israel:

> For though we walk in the flesh, we do not war according to the flesh, for the weapons of our warfare are not of the flesh, but divinely powerful for the destruction of fortresses. We are destroying speculations and every lofty thing raised up against the knowledge of God, and we are taking every thought captive to the obedience of Christ. (2 Cor. 10:3–5)

The Christian's power does not come from the flesh or the material world. We Christians today are often like the Corinthians, who were looking at things as they appear outwardly (2 Cor. 10:7). Our true strength lies in our knowledge and application of God's word to our lives. To take "every thought captive to the obedience of Christ" (2 Cor. 10:5) is to bring our minds in conformity to and subject to Christ's word. God's appointed resource, Scripture, is our only strength, because it is our only weapon that effectively combats evil spiritual forces that attempt to assail the truth of God and drag our faith down. Only God's word and our faith in it can bring light out of darkness, through which the god of this world, Satan, has blinded the minds of the unbelieving (2 Cor. 4:4, 6). Paul describes this spiritual battle further in Ephesians 6:11–13:

> Put on the full armor of God, so that you will be able to stand firm against the schemes of the devil. For our struggle is not against flesh and blood, but against . . . the spiritual forces of wickedness. . . . Therefore, take up the full armor of God, so that you will be able to resist . . . and . . . stand firm.

In Ephesians 6:14–17 are set forth different kinds of spiritual armor with which Christians fight evil. All the armor is defensive in nature except for one offensive weapon: "the sword of the spirit, which is the word of God."

But what does the word of God as our strength have to do with strength coming from weakness? This irony is that God causes situations of physical or material weakness in our lives to motivate us to look to him and his word for sustenance. Without situations of distress, Christians often fail to see their need for God but instead trust in their own natural talents or in some aspect of the world, such as wealth or social relationships. The apostle Paul himself discerned this divine purpose in his own life:

> To keep me from exalting myself, there was given me a thorn in the flesh, a messenger of Satan to torment me—to keep me from exalting myself! Concerning this I entreated the Lord three times that it might leave me. And He has said to me, "My grace is sufficient for you, for power is perfected in weakness." Most gladly, therefore, I will rather boast about my weaknesses, so that the power of Christ may dwell in me. (2 Cor. 12:7–9)

Interpreters have speculated that Paul had malaria or perhaps a severe problem with his eyesight (see 1 Cor. 16:21; Gal. 4:13–15; 5:11). Whatever the problem, it was serious enough that Paul repeatedly prayed for its removal. But while writing to the Corinthians, Paul reflects upon why it came and was not taken away. God caused a physical weakness in Paul so that he would place his trust in God and not in himself. Spiritual power, which grows by our faith in God and his word, can increase only in the soil of our physical, earthly weakness. As one depends on Christ and his word in times of weakness, the Holy Spirit is unleashed to work. Thus Paul links being filled with the Spirit with a person's growth in knowing God's word: "Be filled with the Spirit, speaking to one another in psalms and hymns and spiritual songs" (Eph. 5:18–19).[4]

Consequently, God produces physical or emotional weakness in order that spiritual strength will be produced. He puts us into situations of helplessness and tests us that we may trust him. Our faith will have no opportunity to develop if we are not put into circumstances in which we realize that we need God's aid and must trust him for support. His purpose with us is no different from his purpose with Israel. Moses says to the nation: "[God] humbled you and let you be hungry . . . that He might make you understand that man does not live by bread alone, but man lives by everything that proceeds out of the mouth of the LORD [i.e., his word]" (Deut. 8:3).

God's humbling and testing of Israel in the wilderness was to produce faith in his word to do them good in the end (Deut. 8:16). The New Testament speaks of God testing Christians and Satan tempting them. Interestingly, the word used for God's testing is the very same word employed for Satan's tempting (*peirazō*). This is not coincidental, since God used the same satanic temptations as divine tests for the believer. Satan intends to destroy the saint through tempting, but, ironically, God's purpose is to test for the building up of the Christian's faith. Such ironic testing may best be demonstrated from Christ's temptation in the wilderness. The Gospels explain that Satan "tempted" Jesus (Mark 1:13; Luke 4:13), but Matthew 4:1 adds that "Jesus was *led up by the Spirit* into the wilderness to be tempted by the devil." God meant temptation as a test for Jesus's good, but Satan meant it for evil. Therefore, the same event is used for completely opposite purposes.

Christians likewise encounter ironic testing. God gave Paul a "thorn in the flesh," which Paul understood as "a messenger of Satan,

---

4. The Greek word for "speaking" in Ephesians is an adverbial participle and may indicate either the *means* by which a person is filled with the Spirit or more probably the *result* of being filled with the Spirit. In either case, the "filling with the Spirit" is integrally related to God's word. See the parallel of Col. 3:15–16, which shows this close relationship.

to torment [him]" (2 Cor. 12:7). No doubt, Satan wanted to destroy Paul with this thorn, but God's purpose was to strengthen Paul's faith and to humble him in order that the power of Christ would dwell in him (2 Cor. 12:9).

These ironic temptations and trials occur elsewhere in the Bible (see 1 Cor. 10:13; James 1:1–5, 12; Rev. 2:10). Abraham was "tested" by God in the command to kill his son, but the test was designed only for the upbuilding of his faith in God's promises (Heb. 11:7). Job's experience is a clear example of how God used the temptations of Satan, which Satan hoped would destroy Job's faith, to test Job and to strengthen his trust in God (see Job 1–2). Job apparently discerned this divine purpose:

He knows the way I take;
When He has tried me, I shall come forth as gold.
(Job 23:10)

Though He slay me,
I will hope in Him. (Job 13:15)

Consequently, trials that come from Satan or the world may seem destructive, but God purposes that these same afflictions ultimately prove constructive. In the light of this, we can say with Paul, "Most gladly, therefore, I will rather boast about my weakness, so that the power of Christ may dwell in me. Therefore I am well content with weaknesses, with insults, with distresses, with persecutions, with difficulties, for Christ's sake; for when I am weak, then I am strong" (2 Cor. 12:9–10).

Paul Anderson was frequently billed as the world's strongest man. For many years he traveled around the country giving weight-lifting exhibitions, followed by his personal testimony about faith in Jesus Christ. He often said that physical strength was nothing in comparison to the spiritual strength that Christ could give. Years later Paul Anderson himself suffered from kidney disease, a physical trial that reduced him to a thin, weak man. Yet in an interview toward the end of his life, he testified that his illness had strengthened his faith far more than his physical strength ever had. His faith and spiritual character had more occasion to grow through the testing of ill health than when he was in good health.

The greatest example of power being perfected in weakness is that of the life of Jesus Christ (2 Cor. 13:4). While appearing to be an insignificant peasant during his earthly ministry, Jesus was, in reality, inaugurating the end-time kingdom of God. This inauguration was escalated at his death on the cross, the epitome of weakness. Yet at the point at which he was most weak—death—he was establishing a powerful victory over Satan by taking the punishment of human sin upon himself on behalf of others so they would not have to remain captive to Satan as subjects of his dark kingdom.

Practical Suggestions for Better Understanding and Responding to Suffering

In light of what we have said, Christians should acknowledge the following ironic principles for reacting to suffering.

1. Since our life is to be like Christ's, our life must include suffering of some kind so that God's spiritual strength can be exhibited in our physical weakness.

2. God brings suffering in order to remove anything earthly that we might otherwise be tempted to trust in and to motivate us to look only to him and his word for our sustenance.

3. One key purpose of suffering is to cause us to see our need for God's word, since otherwise faith would not be given opportunity to grow.

4. Our only strength in the midst of suffering lies in knowing, believing, and applying God's word. And it is the Holy Spirit who

gives us strength to trust in God's word in the midst of trials and, in addition, gives us comforting joy at the same time: Paul says to the Thessalonians that "you became imitators of us [apostles] and of the Lord [Jesus], having received the word in much tribulation with the joy of the Holy Spirit" (1 Thess. 1:6; see also Rom. 5:3–5).

5. God takes pleasure in glorifying himself, especially his inscrutable wisdom, by reversing our apparently irreversible situations of defeat into victory.

6. Although many Christians experience victories this side of heaven, all must await the ultimate victory of conquering death through resurrection.

7. God brings the apparent evil of suffering to cause ultimate good for us.

8. God brings the discomfort of our suffering in order that he would comfort and encourage us through it and in order that we would be able in the future to comfort and encourage other believers who go through the same sufferings:

> Blessed be the God and Father of our Lord Jesus Christ, the Father of mercies and God of all comfort, who comforts us in all our affliction so that we will be able to comfort those who are in any affliction with the comfort with which we ourselves are comforted by God. For just as the sufferings of Christ are ours in abundance, so also our comfort is abundant through Christ. But if we are afflicted, it is for your comfort and salvation; or if we are comforted, it is for your comfort, which is effective in the patient enduring of the same sufferings which we also suffer; and our hope for you is firmly grounded, knowing that as you are sharers of our sufferings, so also you are sharers of our comfort. (2 Cor. 1:3–7)

9. Second Corinthians 1:3–6 affirms that the purpose of our sufferings is that God would make us like Christ: "the sufferings of Christ are ours in abundance" (v. 5). Our cruciform life of weakness is the context through which our spiritual strength can be expressed.

10. Second Corinthians 1 also indicates that suffering causes us to realize that we cannot heal or remove suffering from ourselves. Suffering thus brings us to the end of ourselves and leads us to trust in the resources of Christ to heal us. Apart from Christ we are as powerless as dead people. While suffering brings us to the end of ourselves, ironically it causes us to trust in Christ for strength to endure suffering and to be renewed in the living strength of the resurrected Lord:

> For we do not want you to be unaware, brethren, of our affliction which came to us in Asia, that we were burdened excessively, beyond our strength, so that we despaired even of life; indeed, we had the sentence of death within ourselves that we would not trust in ourselves, but in God who raises the dead; who delivered us from so great a peril of death, and will deliver us, He on whom we have set our hope. And He will yet deliver us. (2 Cor. 1:8–10)

These principles must become part of our thinking, or invariably we will react negatively to suffering. The only way to ingrain these maxims is to immerse ourselves on a daily basis in Scripture, through reading and through memorizing and meditating on what we memorize, which are unfortunately forgotten customs in our culture. Scripture gives us an ironic psychology so that we can look positively on suffering.

The application of these principles to Christians suffering persecution in various countries of the world is sometimes easier to see than how they relate to everyday situations in America. Nevertheless, the principles do apply even to apparently mundane circumstances. My wife and I sometimes disagree about issues that are insignificant in the overall scheme of things, such as how to remodel our home. To make matters worse, we both think we are gifted as interior decorators. When I insist on my opinion, she usually hardens in her view, but when I am willing to give in, she becomes more open. The same thing happens when she has insisted on something but then gives in to my view. Mates are to place themselves in a position of weakness toward one another. They are to have an attitude of giving in to the other's desires when apparently irreconcilable conflicts arise. Such weakness is the best way to show spiritual strength and to nurture true relational strength.

This benefit of holding to a posture of weakness does not have its roots in modern psychology. Ephesians 5 shows this posture of weakness through the husband's duty of unconditional sacrifice for the wife: "Husbands, love your wives, just as Christ also loved the church and gave Himself up for her" (v. 25). The same attitude is demonstrated in the wife's submissive, faithful respect for her husband (v. 22). Our culture interprets these roles in Ephesians 5 as postures of weakness, especially the woman's role. From the divine viewpoint—in reality—they are positions of strength. I believe that any healthy psychology of marriage is dependent on this ironic idea.

The same principle is pertinent also to friendships. I find too often that conversation with friends can be dominated by sarcasm. *Sarcasm* comes from a Greek word that means "cutting flesh." Hence we have our colloquial phrase "to cut someone down." I once had a friend who made sarcastic comments about my clothes. If I wore the same pants three times in one week, he would say, "I love your variety in clothes." We have all received these kinds of comments, and I must confess that I have said them to others. When such comments come at me, my typical response is a like sarcasm. Yet I have found that the best way to thwart such offensive "cuts" is with quiet humility and seeming verbal weakness (although this is hard for me to do!).

"Never pay back evil with evil to anyone. . . . Do not be overcome with evil, but overcome evil with good" (Rom. 12:17, 21). We are to reflect Christ: "while being reviled, He did not revile in return; while suffering, He uttered no threats, but kept entrusting Himself to Him who judges righteously" (1 Pet. 2:23). We are to imitate Christ's verbal frailty that concealed spiritual strength.

What is your reaction when you do not receive something you deserve, whether with respect to health, school, sports, job, friendships, or love from another person? Did Christ get what he deserved from this life? In college I was barred from playing in football games for two years because of an obscure NCAA rule that I thought was unfair. Nevertheless, I practiced with the team and prepared myself for the two subsequent years of eligibility. During this waiting period all my energies were geared toward the goal of playing those final two years. The coaches were encouraged about my potential as the time of my eligibility approached. But immediately before my eligibility went into effect, I injured my leg so severely in a practice that I was unable to participate the following year.

Effectively speaking, that was the end of my football career. I asked the Lord why. I could not understand why God would allow my two-year preparation not to come to fruition. As I have reflected on the ironic realities, I have gotten a better perspective. Indeed, that failure in athletics caused me to reflect more on spiritual things than I otherwise would have, and it led me on to seminary, which has been one of the great blessings of my life.

Truly God causes all things to work together for good to those who love him. Why have I intentionally focused on how the principle of irony affects our mundane lives rather than discussing Christians who suffer great calamities? The reason is that God wants Christians to realize that his ironic design of things is just as relevant to everyday affairs as to the greater and more obvious tragic circumstances of life.

5

Faith in Unseen Realities Contradicts Trust in Superficial Appearances

Now faith is the assurance of things hoped for, the conviction of things not seen.

—Hebrews 11:1

I remember the day my wife and I moved into our first house in New England. It was a big house, and there was a huge, beautiful vine growing up one of the exterior corners. We thought the vine made the house look quaint. It wasn't until we had to paint that we found out the hard way that the beautiful vine was poison ivy. Our mistake was depending on superficial appearances and being ignorant of the deeper reality of the ivy leaves. I had to tell my three-year-old son continually that despite appearances the ivy was not a harmless, attractive vine but one that could hurt. He had only my word to go on and the observation of what it had done to his dad's arms. There are many such things in life that appear good but are bad.

On the other hand, there are things that seem bad but are good. The doctors allowed me to witness my wife's second Caesarean operation, when our daughter was born. Excluding gruesome detail, I recall thinking that the large cavity in her stomach certainly didn't *appear* to be good for her! Nevertheless, I had to depend on the doctor's word that regardless of the ugly wound, something beautiful was occurring, and it would all be best for our new baby's health. Later on, I had to trust the doctor's word about my children's welfare when I saw needles stuck into their arms and heard them sob.

Life is packed full of both kinds of inverted realities. The epistle to the Hebrews shows how both types of ironic phenomena apply to the Christian's life of faith in relation to God's word and the world. Hebrews 11 records what has become commonly known as the Old Testament's hall of fame of the faithful. All the characters mentioned have one thing in common: faith in the midst of distress, persecution, and tribulation. Not coincidentally, many of those found in Hebrews 11 have been referenced in previous sections of this book as those who were unjustly victimized by the wicked. However, those oppressors ultimately experienced the very evil they had set out to do to others. We also discover that where there is ironic punishment, there is also often an ironic reward. The latter idea is developed in Hebrews 11, which reveals that the theme we have traced thus far concerning the irony of faith is not unique to the New Testament era. Of course, we have already seen this ironic principle at work in our glimpse at Joseph's life, who also appears in the Hebrews 11 list (v. 22).

Faith in the Midst of Transitoriness

The first character mentioned in Hebrews 11 is Abel. Cain and Abel were the first brothers of the human race, and Cain was the first to commit fratricide. Genesis 4 explains that Abel and Cain both brought offerings before God, but only Abel's was accepted because he offered it in faith. Cain's was rejected because he offered it out of an unbelieving heart (cf. vv. 2–7; Heb. 1:4; 1 John 3:12). In jealous anger Cain murdered Abel and was "cursed from the ground, which has opened its mouth to receive [his] brother's blood" (Gen. 4:11; see also Gen. 3:14, 17–19). This was but evidence that Cain "was of the evil one" (1 John 3:12; see also Gen. 3:14–15), while Abel's faith "obtained the testimony that he was righteous, God testifying about his gifts" (Heb. 11:4). Consequently, Cain's unjust attempt to receive an earthly blessing resulted in his cursing. On the other hand, Abel's enduring faith unto death had its ultimate outcome in life: "Through faith, though he is dead, he still speaks" (Heb. 11:4).

Interestingly, the name Cain in Hebrew is linked with acquisition or possession (Gen. 4:1), while the name Abel (*habel*) literally means breath, vapor, or mist, which elsewhere in the Old Testament denotes what is fleeting or transitory.[1] Could it be that these two brothers had names that pointed subtly to the ironic nature of their character or destiny? For truly Cain tried to *acquire* earthly blessing in the wrong way and was accordingly banished with a curse, being *dispossessed* both physically and spiritually:

> When you cultivate the ground, it will no longer yield its strength to you. . . . You have driven me this day from the face of the ground; and from Your face I will be hidden; and I will be a vagrant and a wanderer on the earth. (Gen. 4:12, 14)

---

1. Cf. K. Seybold, "*hebhel; hābhal*," *Theological Dictionary of the Old Testament* 3 (Grand Rapids, MI: Eerdmans, 1978), 315–20.

And although Abel's name "is intended to signify the breathy character of the fleeting life of the victim,"[2] on the contrary, he was granted eternal life since "through faith, though he is dead, he still speaks." Abel is a model for all believers, for he came to God believing that "He is a rewarder of those who seek Him" (Heb. 11:6), regardless of the cost.

Faith in the Midst of Unbelief

Noah, mentioned in Hebrews 11:7, is also instructive for our theme. When he was born, his father "called his name Noah, saying, 'This one will give us rest from our work and from the toil of our hands arising from the ground which the LORD has cursed'" (Gen. 5:29). The word *Noah* in Hebrew means "rest," from which we can infer that his father's intention in so naming him was to indicate that his child was to bring both rest and comfort to the human race. But the opposite came to pass after Noah was born. Humanity became increasingly wicked, corrupt, and violent, "and the LORD was sorry that He had made man" and decided to blot out and destroy him (see Gen. 6:5–13). The fatherly promise that Noah would bring rest and comfort was fulfilled in mankind's sinful violence and God's sorrow (ironically, the same Hebrew word for comfort in the father's promise is also translated as sorrow in Gen. 6:6–7). Subsequently, God destroyed the earth with a flood.

Therefore, the promised blessing of rest through Noah led to the world's destruction. Even Noah, no doubt, suffered ridicule for building his ark and had to endure the tribulation of the flood, albeit in the ark. Yet God reversed the curse of the restless, turbulent waters into the blessing of rest on dry land: "The ark *rested* upon the mountains of Ararat" (Gen. 8:4). The *rest* of the remnant

---

2. Seybold, "*hebhel; hābhal,*" 316.

human race (Noah's family) is symbolized as Noah offered burnt offerings, and the Lord smelled the "soothing aroma," an expression that comes from a Hebrew term meaning "spirit of rest" (see Gen. 8:20–21).[3]

Noah is a good example of those who faithfully endure tribulation and are rewarded with peace. Noah's faith must have been great, for when he was commanded by God to build the ark, there was no threat of flood, no earthly reason to build a ship. Life continued as normal, just as, from the beginning of creation, they were eating, drinking, marrying, buying, selling, planting, and building (see 2 Pet. 3:4; Luke 17:27–28). Although it did not appear to be the case, the time of judgment was ripening. And Noah expressed his faith by having a "conviction of things not seen" (Heb. 11:1):

> By faith Noah, being warned by God about things *not yet seen*, in reverence prepared an ark for the salvation of his household, by which he condemned the world, and became an heir of the righteousness which is according to faith. (Heb. 11:7)

Noah did not trust his eyes but rather God's word concerning the true nature of reality. The peaceful appearance of the everyday world around him he believed to be a facade, for God had told him that the underlying spiritual reality was unpeaceful and on the brink of catastrophic judgment. He believed the opposite of what appeared to be the case. So it must be with every Christian. God's word is the only true commentary on reality. When we so trust God's word rather than the world's view of itself, we may suffer ridicule and persecution, as Noah did. Peter likely has Noah at least partly in mind when

---

3. For an excellent explanation of the irony involved with Noah's name in Genesis 5–6 see A. P. Ross, "Popular Etymology and Paronomasia in the Old Testament," PhD diss., University of Cambridge (1982), 104–6, upon which the above discussion is based.

he writes, "Keep a good conscience so that in the thing in which you are slandered, those who revile your good behavior . . . will be put to shame" (1 Pet. 3:16, 20–21).

As Noah, so also Christ went against the mainstream of the world's opinion about reality, and because of it also had to suffer many things and be rejected by this generation before he could be glorified (Luke 17:25–26). We as Christians today can also choose no other path. We must insist on God's assessment of reality and approach it from this heavenly ironic viewpoint.

Faith in the Midst of Hopelessness

Abraham, like Noah, is presented in Hebrews 11 as a person who did not trust in physical appearances of the world (Heb. 11:8–15). God had promised to Abraham that through one of his descendants a great nation would arise (Israel), and all the earth would be blessed (see Gen. 12:2–3; 13:16; 15:4–5; 17:2–8). However, most people in Abraham's place would have had a hard time believing this promise, since both Abraham and his wife were childless, very old, and past the age of childbearing: Abraham "contemplated his own body, now as good as dead since he was about a hundred years old, and the deadness of Sarah's womb; yet, with respect to the promise of God, he did not waver in unbelief but grew strong in faith" (Rom. 4:19–20). He believed in God, "who gives life to the dead and calls into being that which does not exist" (4:17). Abraham believed, according to God's promises, in the opposite of what his eyes told him about his and Sarah's childbearing capabilities, so a child, Isaac, was born to the couple.

But God was not finished testing Abraham's faith. God later commanded Abraham to do something quite difficult to understand: "Take now your son . . . and offer him . . . as a burnt offering" (Gen. 22:2). To sacrifice Isaac seemed contradictory, not only in a moral sense, but because God had promised that it would be only through this son of Abraham that a nation would come forth, and all the world would receive a blessing. Nevertheless, Abraham obeyed God's enigmatic command and believed that even if his son were killed, the promises would still somehow be fulfilled through his son:

> By faith Abraham, when he was tested, offered up Isaac, and he who had received the promises was offering up his only begotten son. . . . He considered that God is able to raise people even from the dead, from which he also received him back as a type. (Heb. 11:17, 19)

Indeed, Abraham was "fully assured that what God had promised, He was able also to perform" (Rom. 4:21). Abraham did not trust in *apparent* realities but believed God's word about the truth. Even when God's word *appeared* contradictory, Abraham persisted in faith. Abraham's faith was of an ironic nature, since he believed in the opposite of what his eyes told him.

Indeed, God's promise that Abraham's seed would be multiplied greatly was fulfilled. Abraham's grandson Jacob begot twelve sons, who were subsequently forced to settle in Egypt due to a famine in the land of Canaan. While in Egypt the descendants of the twelve sons grew rapidly into a whole nation, Israel. When the Israelites tried to leave Egypt, they appeared to be headed for destruction under the cruel, tyrannical hand of Pharaoh, yet Pharaoh and his nation were annihilated. Hebrews 11 comments upon this episode. Israel appeared to be headed for drowning in the Red Sea, but the water became land, and Israel escaped; yet when Egypt tried to cross the same land, it was turned to water, and they were trapped in a watery death (Heb. 11:29).

Faith in the Midst of Worldly Pride

Moses's life is especially instructive for learning the ironic recompense of the Christian's faithful life. Exodus 2:1–10 explains how as an infant Moses was delivered from being killed by Pharaoh. Moses's parents placed him in a basket and left it to float on the river, and his sister watched to see what would happen to it. "The irony is that it was Pharaoh's daughter who rescued the infant [from the river] and named him" Moses.[4] Therefore, the very one who delivered Moses's life was the daughter of the very one trying to take his life. "She named him Moses, and said, 'Because I drew him out of the water'" (Ex. 2:10). The Egyptian name of Moses was identical in sound to the Hebrew name that literally meant "drawing out." This one who was drawn out was a foreshadowing of his own future role of drawing out Israel from the Red Sea.[5] This individual who was drawn out was a typological prophecy of the whole nation, which was to be likewise delivered. Moses and Israel certainly demonstrate the general truth that God "sets on high those who are lowly" (Job 5:11).

But Hebrews 11 uncovers even more about Moses, particularly with respect to his personal attitude about life:

> By faith Moses, when he had grown up, refused to be called the son of Pharaoh's daughter, choosing rather to endure ill-treatment with the people of God than to enjoy the passing pleasures of sin, considering the reproach of Christ greater riches than the treasure of Egypt; for he was looking to the reward. By faith he left Egypt, not fearing the wrath of the king; for he endured, *as seeing Him who is unseen.* (vv. 24–27)

---

4. Ross, "Popular Etymology and Paronomasia in the Old Testament," 94.
5. See Ross, "Popular Etymology and Paronomasia in the Old Testament," 94–96, for a good discussion of this aspect of Moses's name, of which my above comments are a summary.

By faith Moses endured earthly suffering, "for he was looking to the reward." He had confidence that if he were faithful, God would "cause all things to work together for good" (Rom. 8:28). Even if his reward did not come in this life, he believed he would receive an eternal reward (Heb. 11:13–16). Although he renounced the visible treasures of Egypt, he possessed invisible, spiritual riches through suffering "the reproach of Christ" (11:26).

Faith in the Midst of Wrath

Another Old Testament example of irony occurs in Hebrews 11:33–34, where we read that by faith some "quenched the power of fire." This reference to fire is likely an allusion to Daniel's friends, Shadrach, Meshach, and Abed-nego. They had refused to worship the false gods of Babylon, especially the novel golden image set up by Nebuchadnezzar (Dan. 3:11–14). As a result, the king decreed that Daniel and his friends be cast into the midst of the furnace of blazing fire (3:20–21). The fire was so hot that it killed the king's servants who threw them into it, yet the three saints were not even singed by the flames. The king responded in astonishment: "Look! I see four men loosed and walking about in the midst of the fire without harm, and the appearance of the fourth is like a son of the gods" (3:25). These godly men certainly didn't place their faith in visible things (Heb. 11:3), but demonstrated their ironic conviction of things not seen (Heb. 11:1) by not compromising and by allowing themselves to be cast into the fire. Rather than trusting their eyes and fearing the visible flames, they placed their confidence in the invisible God. They believed they would be delivered either from physical death or to a "heavenly country" (cf. Dan. 3:17–18; Heb. 11:16). As it was, the Son of God appeared visibly before the eyes of all and delivered them from physical death for a time. Their imminent death was turned by God into an extension of life and, in addition to this, "the king caused Shadrach, Meshach and Abed-nego to prosper" (Dan. 3:30).

Faith in the Midst of Tribulation

The author of Hebrews most certainly had Daniel in mind in mentioning those "who by faith . . . shut the mouths of lions" (Heb. 11:33). Like his three friends, Daniel did not compromise or fear what he saw—the lions—but trusted in the unseen God, who sent his angel to shut the lions' mouths.

And surely when Hebrews mentions that "by faith . . . [some] put foreign armies to flight" (11:33–34), the prophet Elisha is included. At the time that the Assyrian army tried to capture Elisha because of his prophetic abilities, Elisha's servant said, "Alas, my master! What shall we do?" Elisha replied, "Do not fear, for those who are with us are more than those who are with them" (2 Kings 6:15–16). This was hard for the servant to comprehend, since he and Elisha were alone and surrounded by the massive earthly army. By faith Elisha saw the invisible army of the Lord surrounding them. And when Elisha prayed that God would give his servant faith to see the invisible troops, the servant saw that "the mountain was full of horses and chariots of fire all around Elisha" (6:17). This invisible fighting force came down to Elisha and "struck [the Assyrians] with blindness according to the word of Elisha" (6:18). To human eyes, there appeared to be no divine army, but to the eyes of faith the opposite could be seen in the otherwise invisible dimension.

The lives of other faithful saints are summarized in Hebrews 11:34–39. They were people who

> from weakness were made strong. . . . Were tortured, not accepting their [earthly] release, so that they might obtain a better [heavenly] resurrection; and others experienced mockings and scourgings, yes, also chains and imprisonment. They were stoned, they were sawn in two . . . were put to death with the sword; they went about in sheepskins, in goatskins, being destitute, afflicted, ill-treated (men of whom the world was

not worthy), wandering in deserts and mountains and caves and holes in the ground. And all these . . . gained approval through their faith.

Those in Hebrews 11, "of whom the world was not worthy," were thus distinguished from the world by their faith in things not seen through earthly eyes (Heb. 11:1). They "confessed that they were strangers and exiles on the earth. . . . They desire a better country, that is, a heavenly one . . . for [God] has prepared a city for them" (Heb. 11:13, 16). Christians must also live with the same perspective, waiting to "receive a kingdom which cannot be shaken" (Heb. 12:28). "So, let us go out . . . bearing [Jesus's] reproach. For here we do not have a lasting city, but we are seeking the city which is to come" (Heb. 13:13–14). Christians are to put their trust in what God's word says about true reality, which is often the opposite of what the world says and sees of the physical world.

Two categories of ironic redemption in Scripture can be discerned from the examples in Hebrews 11. Believers were delivered in a more overtly miraculous manner (e.g., Daniel and his friends) and in an apparently more natural way (e.g., Joseph). In either case, God is the sole author or cause of rescue, but he uses different means to do so. Perhaps these different methods of ironic blessing can be termed "supernatural providence" and "natural providence."

Of course, ultimately, all deliverances are supernatural in the sense that God is the one causing them to occur, but can believers in the twenty-first century expect their faith to be rewarded by ironic deliverances that occur through supernatural providence? In biblical times, supernatural deliverances certainly seem to have been more prevalent. It is apparent, however, that supernatural redemptions were not the norm even in the biblical era, but they were employed more than in the postbiblical period, leading up to our own contemporary time. In other words, God's natural providence has always been the normative means by which he has worked ironically through events in favor of his saints.

Principles for Faithfulness in the Midst of a Faithless World

From Hebrews 11 we can gather several principles for living in a modern world of unbelief.

1. We live in a world where visible circumstances lure us to do the opposite of what God wills and tempt us to trust in what appears before our eyes (unlike Joseph, who responded well [see Gen. 39]).

2. Appearances are often deceiving, since there is a spiritual reality underlying this physical world (see 2 Kings 6:12–18).

3. A superficial knowledge of Scripture will cause us to be misled about the superficial features of the world (see the implications in 1 Cor. 1:26–2:8; 2 Cor. 5:15–17).

4. We must take radical steps to have a daily dosage of God's word, which reveals the truth of reality (see Rom. 12:2; Col. 3:16).

5. God brings circumstances into our lives that seem to cast doubt on the validity of his word in order to motivate us to live by faith in his word and not by sight (note the case of Abraham [Rom. 4:17–18; Heb. 11:17–19]).

6. Bearing burdensome circumstances by faith is the only exercise causing our spiritually weak muscles to grow strong. Indeed, troublesome times are the God-given opportunities by which we are to develop in maturity (see 2 Cor. 4:16–18; 12:7–10).

Consequently, irony lies at the foundation of our faith, since God's word calls us to believe the opposite of what seems to face us in life. As Paul says:

> Therefore we do not lose heart, but though our outer man
> is decaying, yet our inner man is being renewed day by day.

For momentary, light affliction is producing for us an eternal weight of glory far beyond all comparison, while we look not at the things which are seen, but at the things which are not seen; for the things which are seen are temporal, but the things which are not seen are eternal. . . . For we walk by faith, not by sight. (2 Cor. 4:16–18; 5:7)

Throughout this book I have been emphasizing the importance of Scripture for our lives as Christians. Many of us know the significance of Scripture but we are not consistent in reading and studying it the way we should. Is there a time every day when we read and study Scripture and reflect upon it in prayer? Do we come together as a family and do the same thing? Do we know parts of God's word well enough to think about them during the day's activities? Many of us might give negative answers to some of these questions, and some might respond, "This is fine for preachers and their families but not for 'common Christians.'"

One primary reason that many Christians don't feel the daily necessity for God's word is that we, especially we Americans, are too often enthralled with expectation of the sensational rather than with the uniqueness of the ordinary. We pay attention to TV shows and movies only when the plot has been thrillingly designed to keep our interest at every point. We fritter away much of our day on social media and the Internet. Preachers and teachers lose their audience unless they communicate with melodramatic theatrical skills. We become absorbed in things only when they lure us with excitement, and we are often bored by such ordinary things as sitting down and talking to our mates and our children or taking a walk.

Likewise, if our Bible reading doesn't give us a regular shot of adrenalin, we become easily discouraged and are tempted to forgo consistent reading. Sometimes our reading doesn't seem to uplift us, and other times we don't understand what was read or see how it could ever be applicable. We have deluded ourselves into thinking that only what is exciting—according to our cultural standards—is worthy of our attention and beneficial for us.

We should rather view Scripture reading as an ordinary yet healthy task, like taking vitamins. A few years ago I became ill off and on and continually felt tired. I began taking vitamins with the expectation of feeling better. I decided after about three weeks to quit the vitamins, since I still felt tired. However, I continued to come down with minor ailments. I was expecting a tangible sense of renewed health and vigor, but when it didn't come, I considered the vitamins to be insufficient. Not long after, I discovered that my understanding of how vitamin pills work was deficient. We might never actually feel vitamins working in our body, but as we routinely take them, they build up our immunity. As a result, our strengthened immune system wards off sickness. However, we have to have patient faith that the vitamins are doing their invisible and imperceptible work.

It is the same with Scripture. It may not always intrigue us like an Agatha Christie mystery, or thrill us like a championship victory by our favorite sports team, but it builds up an immunity to sin as we read with patient faith. As a result, this spiritual immune system fights off sinful decisions. Although we may not feel Scripture working in us, we must believe that it is doing an invisible, spiritual work. Over time the consequences will be exciting in the real sense. As the psalmist says, "Your word I have treasured in my heart, that I may not sin against You" (Ps. 119:11).

Indeed, this principle of believing the opposite of what seems to be true is central to the Christian faith. We believe the Holy Spirit is in us even though we cannot perceive him with the five senses. The same is true with the resurrected Jesus in heaven and so many other unseen realities.

6

The Irony of Eschatology

An important strand of irony can be discerned in what is called the "eschatology" of the New Testament. The word *eschatology* comes from two Greek words: (1) *eschatos*, which means "end" or "last," and (2) *logos*, meaning "the study of." Hence *eschatology* means the study of the things pertaining to the end times or last times in the Bible.

An Early-Time View of the End Time

In the early times of Old Testament history there were repeated prophecies of what would occur in the latter times at the end of world history. The phrase "the days to come" (or "the latter days") first occurs in Genesis 49:1 in a prophecy indicating what would happen to the twelve tribes of Israel. One of the main aspects of the prophecy is to foretell the coming of the Messiah from the tribe of Judah, who is likened to a lion:

> The scepter shall not depart from Judah,
> Nor the ruler's staff from between his feet,

> Until Shiloh comes,
> And to him shall be the obedience of the peoples. (Gen. 49:10)

It is clear from this passage that this coming messianic ruler will begin to reign through his judgment of the wicked nations (see vv. 11–12).[1] Thus, Genesis 49 speaks of a messianic ruler who will make his appearance "in the latter days."[2]

Numbers 24 continues the prophetic theme and again reveals what will happen "in the days to come" (v. 14):

> A star shall come forth from Jacob,
> A scepter shall rise from Israel,
> And shall crush through the forehead of Moab. . . .
> One from Jacob shall have dominion. (vv. 17–19)

The prophecy has the same focus as that of Genesis: a coming messianic ruler from Israel who will judge evil nations and exercise his reign in the latter days.[3]

Similarly, Isaiah 2:2 speaks of the Lord's mountain temple being established "in the last days" (see also Mic. 4:1–3). At this time, "na-

---

1. The figures of speech in vv. 11–12 denote violent defeat, which is borne out further by the similar use of the same figures in Isa. 63:2–4, 6.

2. Some scholars assert that the phrase "in the latter days" (or "latter days") in Gen. 49:1 refers only to the indefinite future within the scope of the author. However, that the phrase has a much more distant meaning should be evident from the prophecy that to the coming king of Judah will "be the obedience of the peoples" (Gen. 49:10), which receives confirmation from the New Testament understanding of Gen. 49:9–10 (and our following discussion). For example, Paul identifies "Shiloh" with Jesus Christ, who brought about "the obedience of the Gentiles" (Rom. 15:18; cf. also 1:5, 16:26), and Rev. 5:5 also identifies "the lion that is from the tribe of Judah" with Jesus. On this see further G. K. Beale, *A New Testament Biblical Theology* (Grand Rapids, MI: Baker, 2011), 92–99.

3. See further Beale, *New Testament Biblical Theology*, 99–101. That the prophecy of Numbers 24 also goes beyond the immediate purview of the author is evident from an allusion to part of its fulfillment in Dan. 11:30, which refers to prophesied events in Num. 24:24 that were to occur during a period directly associated with the end time (Dan. 11:40) and "the latter days" (Dan. 10:14). Of course, the context of Daniel 11 is overtly eschatological and, as is well known, relates to the coming of the Messiah and the destruction and judgment of evil (see Dan. 7–9 and 12). The Numbers 24 prophecy also develops that of Genesis 49 (note the common uses of "scepter," latter days, and the phrase "he crouches, he lies down as a lion, and as a lion who dares rouse him up?" [Gen. 49:9 and Num. 24:9], which describes an Israelite messianic-like military leader).

tion will not lift up sword against nation, and never again will they learn war" (Isa. 2:4). Hosea 3:5 adds to Isaiah's prophecy and states that "in the last days" not only will the Lord reign, but there will also be a Davidic king ruling with him.

Two other significant references to the latter days in the Old Testament occur in the book of Daniel. First, King Nebuchadnezzar has a dream of "what will take place in the latter days" (2:28). In this dream he sees a great statue composed of four different metals, which is destroyed by a single stone. The interpretation of the dream reveals that the four metallic sections of the statue represent four great world kingdoms that will follow one after another. All of these kingdoms will be destroyed by God. The focus and climax of the dream is that at the end of the latter days—the end-time—the last (fourth) world kingdom will be destroyed and God's eternal kingdom will be established.

In the second occurrence, in Daniel 10:14, the reference to the latter days also concerns the rise and fall of world powers leading up to "the end time," when the last evil world ruler will be judged and the righteous delivered (see also Dan. 11:40–12:3).

Though there are other uses of the phrase "latter days" in the Old Testament, we may conclude from this brief survey that the idea of the latter days in the Old Testament primarily refers to the coming establishment of God's eternal kingdom, especially as that kingdom is set up by the Messiah.[4] The "latter days" may be a broader period than often thought by some contemporary commentators (such as Hal Lindsey),[5] but its focus is on the final defeat of evil and setting up of God's permanent rule. Furthermore, almost all of the above passages

---

4. The phrase "latter days" also has an eschatological meaning in Ezek. 38:16, where it pertains to the end-time tribulation, which Israel must endure. For a more thorough study surveying more of the uses of the phrase "latter days" in the Old Testament, see Beale, *New Testament Biblical Theology*, 88–116.

5. E.g., like Hal Lindsey, *The Late Great Planet Earth* (Grand Rapids, MI: Zondervan, 1970), who views the end times to begin only with the church's future rapture, followed by the great tribulation and Christ's purported millennial reign.

apparently foresee God destroying the kingdoms of evil and setting up his own kingdom by outward force. This is why later Jewish interpreters of these and similar Old Testament prophecies portray the Messiah as a military conqueror who defeats Israel's enemy in battle.

That the Messiah was predominantly thought of as a military leader who would conquer Israel's oppressors is apparent from a brief survey of passages in early Jewish writings. Daniel 2 and 7 were influential in molding such thought about a future deliverer. A Jewish author in a work known as *4 Ezra* (written around AD 100) explains that the events recorded in Daniel 2 and 7 would occur in "the last days."[6] The author of *4 Ezra* identifies the Son of Man from Daniel 7 with the "stone" of Daniel 2, which destroyed the four kingdoms symbolized by the great statue (cf. *4 Ezra* 13:1–12). The author then speculates about how he thinks the Son of Man will destroy the wicked in the last days. He claimed to foresee in a visionary dream quite a supernatural, military show of strength:

> There was gathered together . . . a multitude of men to make war against the Man [Son of Man]. . . . When he saw the assault of the multitude . . . he sent out of his mouth as it were a fiery stream, and out of his lips a flaming breath . . . and [it] fell upon the assault of the multitude . . . and burned them up. (*4 Ezra* 13:5–11)

Although this may be a metaphorical picture of how the Messiah was to defeat the wicked, it nonetheless refers to some kind of forceful destruction.[7]

---

6. For the phrase and its synonyms see *4 Ezra* 11:39; 11:59; 12:9, 23, 29, 32; 13:19, 27, 47). The Jewish writings discussed here and in the remainder of this section are not contained in the canon of the Bible but were written directly preceding, during, or soon after the first century AD. These writings reflect the thoughts and beliefs of the Jewish people at the time.

7. Cf. *4 Ezra* 13:37–38 with *4 Ezra* 11:37 and 12:31–36, where the same destruction is portrayed.

Another source that reflects Jewish messianic thought in the first century is *2 Baruch*, which also speaks of the forceful rule of the Messiah:

> The last [wicked] leader of that time will be left alive, when the multitude of his hosts will be put to the sword and he will be bound . . . and My Messiah will convict him of all his impurities . . . and afterwards he will put him to death. (*2 Bar.* 40:1–2)

According to the author of *2 Baruch*, this destruction will take place in "the last time" (*2 Bar.* 41:6). The same writer further emphasizes this by saying that at "the ends of the times and . . . the consummation, moreover, of the age shall then show the great might of its ruler, when all things come to judgment" (*2 Bar.* 83:6–7). And according to another Jewish writer there shall

> come from the plains of heaven *a blessed man* [no doubt, the Messiah] with the sceptre in his hand which God has committed to his clasp: and he has won fair dominion over all, and . . . he has destroyed every city from its foundations . . . and burnt up all the families of men who before wrought evil. (*Sibylline Oracles*, book 5, lines 414–19)

The judgment performed by this "blessed man" is understood by this author to take place "in the last time."[8] This popular conviction of the coming Messiah's military overthrow of the forces of evil was widespread.[9] In fact, members of the well-known community of Qumran near the Dead Sea even wrote a book called *The War of the Sons of Light against the Sons of Darkness*. The book was composed

---

8. See *The Sibylline Oracles*, book 5, lines 348, 361, and 432.

9. The conviction was held at least as early as the second century BC (e.g., see 1 Enoch 90:6–18).

of military regulations for how the righteous should conduct the final battle against the wicked at the end of time.[10]

Other Jewish writings of the first centuries BC and AD reflect the same militaristic view of the Messiah and defeat of God's enemies. Therefore, there was a consensus of Jewish thought at this time that understood the Old Testament prophecies of the latter days to refer to the forceful overthrow of wicked world rulers by the Messiah and the subsequent establishment of God's kingdom on earth.

However, the writings in *4 Ezra*, *2 Baruch*, and Qumran are especially significant because they speculate specifically about how in particular the "latter day" prophecies of Daniel 2; 7; and 10–12 are going to be fulfilled.[11] We will see the significance of this directly.

The Kingdom of the End Times:
The Best of Times, the Worst of Times

Charles Dickens's well-known novel *A Tale of Two Cities* takes place during the turbulent days before and during the French Revolution. The opening paragraph of the book characterizes the paradoxical nature of that troublesome period:

> It was the best of times, it was the worst of times, it was the age of wisdom, it was the age of foolishness, it was the epoch of belief, it was the epoch of incredulity, it was the season of Light, it was the season of Darkness, it was the spring of hope, it was the winter of despair, we had everything before us, we

10. See column 1 of the Qumran *War Scroll*, which is a meditation based on Daniel 11–12. The first section of the book repeatedly speaks of the "time" when the battle will occur. The same Hebrew word for "time" occurs in the latter chapters of the *War Scroll*.

11. For discussion supporting this contention see my book, *The Use of Daniel in Jewish Apocalyptic Literature and in the Revelation of St. John* (Washington, DC: University Press of America, 1984), 42–66, 112–153; see the same pages in Beale, *Use of Daniel*, for further discussion of the above Jewish passages and messianic notions. Other Jewish writings that see a forceful overthrow by the Messiah are *1 En.* 90:6–18; 46–48 and the *Testament of Joseph* 19:6–12. This overthrow is seen as taking place in the end times, although these texts do not use any such overt eschatological phrases to denote this.

had nothing before us, we were all going direct to Heaven, we were all going direct the other way.

Dickens accurately captures the irony of that stormy period. It seemed that all was well with the French monarchy, but, in reality, it was about to be overthrown. Immediately before the Revolution, France was a symbol of all that the Enlightenment or the Age of Reason stood for: rationality, order, decorum, stability. But an age of foolishness was about to dawn on the unsuspecting nation in the form of a chaotic rebellion. France had also been one of the strongholds of the Catholic faith, but the Revolution was against all forms of Christian belief.

Dickens's introductory words are an equally appropriate description of the ironic times of the first century AD in which Christ lived and died. Truly the Jews felt these were the *worst of times* because of Rome's harsh domination over Israel, but it was really the *best of times* because God was entering the world to save man from a much harsher rule than Rome, the dominion of Satan himself. Many Jews considered this period in Palestine to be the Jewish age of wisdom, but they were to demonstrate their ultimate foolishness by rejecting their own Messiah. It was the season of darkness, yet a great light shone in its midst. Certainly most Jews, like Paul, thought they were all going "direct to heaven, but ironically were all going direct the other way."

The Jews thought it was the worst of times because they failed to discern the signs of the end times, which were harbingers of the best of times. That is, they did not perceive that Jesus was their long-promised Messiah. Therefore, for the majority of the Jews in the first century and for Jews up until our own time, the end times have not yet arrived because the Messiah has not yet come to destroy the wicked world rulers and has not yet inaugurated the best of times, which is his kingdom of universal peace. The New Testament writers, however, believed that the end times had begun in their own generation! Peter declares that the Christian's redemption has *already* taken place "in these last times for the sake of you who through Him are believers in God, who raised Him from the dead and gave Him glory" (1 Pet. 1:20–21). In other words, the Old Testament prophecies about the latter days were beginning to be fulfilled but not through an overturning of earthly military oppressors. Indeed, the end times were beginning through Christ's spiritual defeat of the invisible forces of evil. We already discussed in some depth how Christ ironically defeated satanic forces spiritually by allowing himself to be nailed to the cross, and it is in this ironic manner that the end times begin.

Consequently, the end times or latter days, contrary to popular Jewish hopes, does not refer initially to a blissful period when all of God's enemies are completely exterminated and God's eternal kingdom is established throughout the earth. Rather, this initial eschatological period refers to an ironic time when an invisible victory is won at the cross over Satan and his kingdom. What appeared to be the worst of times for Christ as he was crucified was, instead, the best of times. Ironically, as evil forces seem to be winning victories on earth, they are, in reality, losing spiritual battles. When the forces of God appear to be losing physical battles, they are really winning in the spiritual realm. For the majority of Jews, if the first century in which they lived was the beginning of the end times, it was certainly the *opposite* of what they had come to believe the end times would bring. They were too wise to believe such foolishness. This, no doubt, is why so many refused to acknowledge Jesus as Messiah and would not believe that the well-known latter days prophesied in the Old Testament had begun.

But the earliest Jewish Christian leaders were adamant that Jesus's ironic victory at the cross and subsequent resurrection had inaugurated the end-time kingdom. Jesus himself said, "The *time* is fulfilled, and the kingdom of God is at hand" (Mark 1:15). The author of Hebrews refers to Christ's first coming as happening "in these last days," at which time "He had made purification of sins" (Heb. 1:2–3).[12] Therefore, for many in Jesus's day the "latter days" had come too early to warrant belief. However, the Jews were not completely wrong. There will come a time at the very end of world history when the Messiah will physically conquer and establish an earthly kingdom, but not now in the church age leading up to that time.

The Irony of Christ's End-Time Kingdom

We have already discussed at some length how Jesus ironically began to fulfill the Daniel 7 prophecy of a "Son of Man" who would come and rule over all the earth.[13] Through his suffering and death, Jesus began to reign spiritually over Satan and his demonic forces. At the time of his first coming, he did *not* rule physically. Therefore, the prophecy in Daniel 7 concerning a messianic "Son of Man" who would come and rule over the earth was fulfilled initially in Christ's ironic rule through suffering during his earthly ministry and his apparent defeat at the cross.

In the book of Daniel this prophecy of the Son of Man's kingdom was to be inaugurated in the latter days. This is clear from Daniel 2, where "in the latter days" (v. 28) a stone cut out without hands was to destroy a huge statue representing four evil empires of the world. Most scholars agree that the judgment of these four wicked kingdoms in Daniel 2 parallels the judgment of the same four world empires in Daniel 7 (vv. 1–12). Although Daniel 7 does not say explicitly that the Son of Man is the one who judges these satanically

---

12. See likewise Heb. 9:26 and Gal. 4:4–5. Cf. also 1 John 2:18, which speaks of John's readers as living in "the last hour."

13. See chapter 3 of this book.

inspired kingdoms, it is implied, for immediately after their destruction the Son of Man is enthroned as world ruler (vv. 13–14). The four kingdoms that are to be destroyed refer to Babylon, Medo-Persia, Greece, and Rome. But how could Christ, the Son of Man, destroy all four of these empires through his one spiritual victory at the cross? The beginning answer lies in the scriptural fact that all four of these empires had Satan as their ultimate ruler (see, e.g., Matt. 4:8–9; 2 Cor. 4:4). Accordingly, when Jesus, the stone of Daniel 2:34–35, defeated Satan at the cross, he defeated the then contemporary world power, Rome, as well as the previous three world kingdoms. This is well-symbolized in Daniel 2:34–35, where the stone smashes the huge statue composed of four metals representing the four kingdoms.

Therefore, the rock of Daniel 2 and Son of Man of Daniel 7 refer prophetically to Jesus and his defeat of evil "in the latter days," when he will also establish his cosmic kingdom.[14] This latter-day kingdom began ironically on an invisible level in the first century but will climax at the end of world history manifestly before all eyes.

The Emperor's Invisible Clothes:
Christ's End-Time Kingdom in the Book of Revelation

One of Hans Christian Andersen's most humorous tales is *The Emperor's New Clothes*. An unwise king spent all the money in his treasury for new clothes because he always liked to wear something new and different. One day two sly crooks who knew his weakness approached him and said that they could weave the world's most elegant clothes on their special looms. However, they also explained that the new garments would have the magical quality of being invisible to anyone who was unworthy of his office. When the two

---

14. Even the Jews of Jesus's day identified the Son of Man of Daniel 7 with the "stone" of Daniel 2 (e.g., *4 Ezra* 13:1–13). Jesus likewise refers to himself not only as Son of Man but also as the Daniel 2 "stone," albeit much less frequently (cf. Matt. 21:44; Luke 20:18).

conmen claimed to have finished weaving the new clothes, the king's officials inspected them. Although they could see nothing, they reported to the king that the clothes were beautiful, since they were fearful to do otherwise because they might be considered unworthy of their position in the king's service. For the same reason, when the king was shown the imaginary clothing, he praised them as the work of artisans even though he saw nothing. The king then wore his new clothes in a glorious procession through the streets, and the crowd praised his clothes for the same reasons as before. Finally, a small boy shouted out that the emperor had no clothes on, and everyone including the king realized the truth.

In a somewhat similar yet completely different way, Jesus Christ is the emperor who had his clothes stripped from him on the cross, yet at the same time was clothed spiritually with invisible royal robes symbolic of his ironic kingship. Indeed, whereas the clothes of the foolish king in Andersen's tale were not only invisible but imaginary, Christ's were invisible but spiritually real. To the earthly eyes of the Jews, Jesus appeared as a naked criminal, but to the heavenly eyes of faith he was a king clothed in spiritual power. The book of Revelation reveals in some depth a heavenly interpretation of Christ's uncovered body on the cross and of his resurrection. Therefore, to this last book of Scripture we must turn to discover further the irony of Christ's death and of his heavenly rule throughout the church age.

The word *revelation* or *apocalypse* comes from a Greek term meaning unveil, uncover, or reveal. This is why the last book of the Bible is called the "Revelation of Jesus Christ" or the "Apocalypse of Jesus Christ" (Rev. 1:1). This book uncovers for us a heavenly interpretation of earthly events. *The* event upon which Revelation primarily focuses is Christ's death and resurrection and its effects upon mankind. The book of Revelation does not assert anything completely new beyond what the rest of the New Testament writers already say about the irony concerning Christ's death and its implications, but it does expand upon this theme. We are shown more fully how the irony of Christ's eschatological kingship relates to the life of the Christian believer. Therefore, although Revelation has much to say about the future, it has much to say also about the past and the present.[15]

But there must be a preliminary discussion before we can understand what Revelation affirms about the end-time kingdom. As we have already seen, the book of Daniel is indispensable to a proper view of what Christ meant when he so often referred to himself in his earthly ministry as the Son of Man.[16] Likewise, the central truths of Revelation cannot be comprehended adequately without a knowledge of the book of Daniel, since Daniel is one of the most important and pervasive influences throughout this last book of the Bible.[17] In particular, as in the case with the Gospels, so with Revelation the picture of Daniel 7 is crucial. Verses 13–14 of Daniel 7 especially deserve repeated attention here:

> I [Daniel] kept looking in the night visions,
> And behold, with the clouds of heaven
> One like a Son of Man was coming,
> And He came up to the Ancient of Days
> And was presented before Him.
> And to Him was given dominion,
> Glory and a kingdom,

---

15. With respect to the time-scope of Revelation see G. K. Beale, *The Book of Revelation* (Grand Rapids, MI: Eerdmans, 1999), 108–70, and my article "The Influence of Daniel upon the Structure and Theology of John's Apocalypse," *Journal of the Evangelical Theological Society* 27 (1984): 413–23.

16. See chapter 3 of this book

17. For demonstration of this assertion see my book *Use of Daniel*, 154–328. For a fuller discussion of John's eschatological understanding of Daniel see my article "The Influence of Daniel upon the Structure and Theology of John's Apocalypse," 415–20.

That all the peoples, nations and men of every language
Might serve Him.
His dominion is an everlasting dominion
Which will not pass away.

The words "One like a Son of Man was coming, and He came up to the Ancient of Days and was presented before Him" refer to the enthronement procession of the Son of Man. We have seen that while Daniel's prophecy appears to describe the Messiah's entrance up to the divine throne as occurring very briefly and majestically, the Gospels show in detail exactly how this prophesied entrance was fulfilled: Christ's approach to the throne consisted of his three-year ministry, which was characterized by suffering, poverty, and humility, and climaxed by his death and ascension to heaven at the right hand of God's throne.

The emphasis of the Gospels is upon the extended duration of Jesus's ironic procession leading up to his heavenly enthronement. On the other hand, the emphasis of John's Revelation is upon Jesus's ironic enthronement when he ascended into heaven as a result of his victorious death. Jesus's death on the cross was the transition from his humble procession to his enthronement in majesty. This death was an unseen victory over Satan and sin that was verified as such by the resurrection and ascension. The only passageway to enthronement was through the way of the cross.

The first verses of Revelation describe how Jesus ironically gains his kingship through the suffering of death: "Jesus Christ, the faithful witness, the firstborn of the dead, and the ruler of the kings of the earth" (Rev. 1:5). Although Jesus's kingship cannot be seen with the naked eye and is unrecognized by the world's rulers, he nonetheless rules over them in an invisible, spiritual manner and accomplishes his sovereign will through them (see Rev. 17:16–17). Part of the irony is that even though he does not appear to be ruling over evil world tyrants, he actually is at every moment. The Gospels depict the Son of Man's royal identity as veiled by the clothing of humble humanity, while Revelation portrays the same identity of the Son of Man as hidden by a heavenly cloak. For example, in Revelation 1:13 Jesus is pictured as enthroned in heaven "like a son of man, clothed in a robe reaching to the feet, and girded across His chest with a golden sash." As in Jesus's earthly ministry, only the eye of faith could perceive the majestic identity of the suffering Son of Man; likewise only faith can penetrate the heavenly curtain and see Christ sitting in a majestic robe at the right hand of his Father's throne. At this time Jesus was "crowned with glory and honor" (Heb. 2:9), but the eye of unbelief is blinded from seeing it. Although Jesus's majestic garb is thought by some to be imaginary, it is nonetheless real. "The heavens were opened" only to genuine faith so that Christ's sovereignty over earthly affairs can be understood clearly (cf. Ezek. 1:1; Rev. 4:1).

As already mentioned, Daniel foretold that his prophecies would be fulfilled in the "latter days" (Dan. 2:28; 10:14) or in the "time of the end" (Dan. 8:17, 19; 11:27, 35, 40; 12:4, 9). Since Jesus's death, resurrection, and ascension began to fulfill the prediction in Daniel 7:13–14, that one like a Son of Man would be given dominion, glory, and a kingdom, it is clear that John understood the end times spoken of through Daniel as beginning with Christ's first coming. And this eschatological period would continue on the earth and in heaven until Christ's second coming. Yet most Jews could not believe that the long-awaited eschatological kingdom of the Messiah had arrived because of their inability to perceive its ironic nature. They lived by sight and not by faith. They could not bring themselves to believe the opposite of what their eyes told them—that the crucified and barely clothed Jesus was actually their king and had ascended into heaven and was clothed with glory in order to reign at God's right hand.

Hence, for such people the doors of heavenly realities were closed. But the keys of heaven's doors were given to those faithful ones whom the Jews persecuted. So, for instance, as Stephen was being stoned to death by the Jews, he exclaimed, "I see the heavens opened up and the Son of Man standing at the right hand of God" (Acts 7:56). Ironically, Stephen (which means "crowned one") was about to be crowned because of his faithfulness to death, as he trod the same path which his Lord had—from suffering to majestic glory. Similarly, the apostle John saw "a door standing open in heaven" through which he beheld the enthroned Lamb because he was by faith a fellow partaker in the tribulation and kingdom and perseverance which are in Christ Jesus (see Rev. 1:9; 4:1; 5:6). Although he had suffered due to his testimony of Jesus, he was rewarded with eyes to see the true kingly status of his crowned Lord in heaven (see Rev. 1:9, 12; 4:1; 5:6).

The Shepherd's Ironic Iron Staff

Jesus's establishment of the end-time kingdom through death and resurrection is a fulfillment of numerous other Old Testament prophecies in addition to that of Daniel's Son of Man. In Revelation 2 Christ's first coming is also explained as a fulfillment of the messianic prophecy in Psalm 2. This psalm foretells a period when God's "Son" (v. 7) and "Messiah" (v. 2) will reign as "King" (v. 6). At this time God will address his son in order to explain the nature and extent of his imminent rule:

> I will surely give the nations as Your inheritance,
> And the very ends of the earth as Your possession.
> You shall break them with a rod of iron,
> You shall shatter them like earthenware. (Ps. 2:8–9)

These verses describe two things about the coming Messiah's rule. First, it will be a universal, worldwide rule. Second, the Messiah will have to defeat an enemy before establishing his kingdom. The Jews believed that this prophecy would be fulfilled only in a literal, physical manner. In fact, one Jewish writer in the first century BC understood the future fulfillment of Psalm 2:8–9 in the following manner:

> Behold, O Lord, and raise up unto them their king, the Son of David . . . that he may reign over Israel Thy servant. And gird him with strength, that he may shatter unrighteous rulers, and that he may purge Jerusalem from nations that trample [her] down to destruction. . . . He shall thrust out sinners from [the] inheritance, he shall destroy the pride of the sinner as a potter's vessel. With a rod of iron he shall break in pieces all their substance, he shall destroy the godless nations with the word of his mouth; at his rebuke nations shall flee before him (*Pss. Sol.* 17:21–25).[18]

In Revelation 2:26–27 John too refers to Psalm 2, but his understanding of it is much different from the predominant Jewish view:

> He who overcomes, and he who keeps My deeds until the end, *to him I will give authority over the nations; and he shall rule them with a rod of iron, as the vessels of the potter are broken to pieces*, as I also have received authority from My Father. (Italic type represents a quotation from the Old Testament)

John is quoting Psalm 2:8–9 and applying it to the lives of Christians. Of course, Jesus is the one actually quoting the psalm, and John is recording Jesus's words.

---

18. For a similar Jewish view of Psalm 2 at the end of the first century AD, see *4 Ezra* 13:32–38.

What does Christ mean by applying the prophecy from Psalm 2 to the lives of Christians? This is a crucial question, since the psalm is a prophecy of how the Messiah will reign over a world kingdom, and there is no reference to saints reigning with him. Jesus's intent is to tell Christians that if they persevere in their faith until death, they will be rewarded by reigning with Jesus over a kingdom that he has already established. At the end of Revelation 2:27 Jesus affirms that he has begun to fulfill the psalm's prophecy of a messianic rule. After saying that Christians can receive the ruling power promised in Psalm 2, Christ tells them on what basis they will be able to obtain it—"as I also have received authority from my Father." That is, he has begun to fulfill the Psalm 2:8–9 prophecy in the past, and, because of this, Christians who are in union with him will also be enabled to reign with him in the future.

Christ began to fulfill the Psalm 2 prophecy even before the end of the first century AD. We see how Jesus fulfilled this prophecy when we compare Psalm 2 to John's quotation of it in Revelation 2. The observant reader will notice that there is a crucial difference between the wording of Psalm 2:9 and John's allusion to it in Revelation 2:27:

Psalm 2:9	Revelation 2:27
Thou shalt *break* them with a staff of iron.	He shall *shepherd* them with a staff of iron.

Where the psalm has "break," Revelation reads "shepherd" (NASB translates this as "rule"). Some scholars have said that the alteration is due merely to a mistaken translation on John's part.[19] However, this option is unacceptable to those who hold to the divine inspiration

---

19. E.g., see the discussion of G. B. Caird, *The Revelation of St. John* (New York: Harper & Row, 1966), 45–46.

of Scripture. The original Hebrew word in Psalm 2 could legitimately be translated either as "break" *or* as "shepherd," and possibly both meanings were originally in mind. That is, Psalm 2 and Revelation 2 are portraying the image of a shepherd with an iron staff. In the psalm the Messiah is the shepherd who has authority to wield the staff, and in Revelation Christ is seen as the fulfillment of the Messiah who has received authority from his Father to take up the staff. The shepherd's staff may well have an ironic purpose in both passages: to those trusting in the Messiah, it is a staff of protection by which they are tenderly shepherded; but to those in rebellion, the same iron staff becomes a weapon by which the shepherd destroys them. Hence, the best translation in the two passages is "shepherd" with an ironic nuance.

In light of the coming of Christ, John understands this irony in a fuller way than did the psalmist. Christ's cross is now understood as (or, at least, included as) what the iron staff represents—the cross, or staff, protects those trusting in it, yet, ironically, the very same staff condemns and judges those rejecting it. Furthermore, whereas the psalm *appears* to say that the messianic shepherd will conquer by forcefully destroying the wicked in a physical manner, John sees Jesus's conquering of the enemy through spiritual means. Jesus spiritually conquered Satan and the satanic hosts by allowing them to conquer him physically. In this last sense, Christ *began* to fulfill the Psalm 2 prophecy in an ironic manner, but at his second coming he will fulfill it more literally, as all of his enemies will be defeated both physically and spiritually.[20]

---

20. This shepherding irony in both Ps. 2 and Rev. 2 has already been observed in the nineteenth century by E. W. Hengstenberg, *The Revelation of St. John*, vol. 1 in Clark's Foreign Theological Library (Edinburgh: T. & T. Clark, 1851), 461, and more recently by J. P. M. Sweet, *Revelation* (London: SCM Press, 1979), 96. A very similar view is held by R. Jamison, A. R. Fausset, and D. Brown, *A Commentary: Critical, Practical and Explanatory on the Whole Bible: New Testament, vol. 2, Galatians–Revelation* (Toledo, OH: Jerome B. Names, 1884), 528–29. The Hebrew word *t'rm* in Ps. 2:9 seems to come from *r'h* ("to shepherd") rather than *r''* ("to break"). The rendering of "shepherd" is supported by the Greek Old Testament (LXX), which gave the same translation of Ps. 2:9 at least two centuries before the time of Christ. If the translation of

Christ: The End-Time King

Indeed, the Messiah's end-time kingdom foretold in the Old Testament began to be fulfilled in Christ's death, resurrection, and ascension. John reaffirms this idea in a way similar to his previous allusion to the shepherd's iron staff in Psalm 2: "He who overcomes [conquers], I will grant to him to sit down with Me on My throne, as I also overcame and sat down with My Father on His throne" (Rev. 3:21). The concept here is almost identical to that in Revelation 2:26–27. Again, Jesus is promising believers that if they overcome (persevere in faith through earthly tribulations), they will be able to reign with him at some future point. They are promised a future reign *on the basis* that Christ himself has already established a spiritual kingdom and begun to reign in heaven.

Revelation 5:5–7 explains in more detail the precise manner in which Jesus inaugurated his dominion. In verse 5 John hears a heavenly voice saying that Jesus is a lion who has conquered. But when John sees a vision of this divine conqueror, in verse 6, he sees only "a Lamb standing, as if slain." Why is there such a difference in what John *hears* about Christ as a conqueror and what he *sees*? The lion image in verse 5 comes from Genesis 49:9, where the Messiah is portrayed as apparently destroying his enemies in a physical manner. However, the "slain lamb" picture (also from the Old

---

"break" is preferred, which is possible, then the irony might disappear from Ps. 2, and John would not be seen as interpreting the psalm in an ironic way. Alternatively, the psalmist may have intended the ambiguity between the two words, again, for ironic purposes.

  Another interpretation of the verb "to shepherd" in Rev. 2:27 sees it as synonymous with "smite" (or "destroy"), since it is in parallelism with such a word in Rev. 19:15. This meaning is seen to be further supported by observing that the Greek verb "to shepherd" (*poimainō*) can sometimes mean "destroy" in the Greek Old Testament (for this view see S. L. Johnson, *The Old Testament in the New* [Grand Rapids, MI: Zondervan, 1980], 19). Even if the meaning of "destroy" is preferred in Rev. 2:27, the image of a shepherd's staff is still retained and, hence, the irony could still be in mind, i.e., the staff which destroys, at the same time also protects. In fact, the same kind of irony is in mind in at least one of the three places in the Old Testament where it is argued that the verb *poimainō* means "destroy" (see Mic. 5:6 and its context). See G. K. Beale, *Revelation*, 266–68, for fuller explanation and discussion of the various interpretive options for the use of Ps. 2:9 in Rev. 2:27.

Testament, Isa. 53) *interprets* this messianic prophecy by showing that the Messiah's conquering of evil was to begin in an ironic and spiritual manner. So again we see that Jesus began to win a victory over Satan and his forces spiritually through permitting himself to be slain physically by them at the cross.

That the cross itself was a victory, even before the resurrection, is clear from Revelation 5:9–10, where Christ is said to have purchased with his blood at the cross "men from every tribe and tongue and people and nation" and had "made them to be a kingdom" (see also Rev. 1:5–6). All of this was ironically accomplished by his death but was guaranteed to be effectual by his subsequent resurrection. The irony of Jesus's ascended condition is stressed by the portrayal of "a Lamb standing, as if slain." He was *slain*, yet he was made to *stand* through the resurrection. He appears as slaughtered yet, at the same time, he is standing strong. About the seemingly contradictory juxtaposition of lion and lamb images in Revelation 5:5–6 G. B. Caird has well said:

> It is almost as if John were saying to us . . . "Wherever the Old Testament says 'Lion,' read 'Lamb.'" Wherever the Old Testament speaks of the victory of the Messiah or the overthrow of the enemies of God, we are to remember that the gospel recognizes no other way of achieving these ends than the way of the cross.[21]

Of course, Jesus's ironic victory in death was completed by his resurrection and exaltation to life (see Rev. 5:7). Caird's words should also be qualified by a reiteration that John sees a day at the very end of world history in which Christ *will* physically and spiritually judge the wicked.

---

21. Caird, *Revelation of St. John*, 75.

The Knights of the Cross and Their End-Time Battle

The plot of Cervantes's novel *Don Quixote de la Mancha* has intrigued readers for centuries. Don Quixote is an old man who read so many books about heroic knights and their chivalry that he thought about nothing else. Finally, he decided to imitate some of these legendary knights and to revive the institution of knighthood. After obtaining some rusty old armor and a skinny horse, he rode out to find people in distress who needed the deliverance of a gallant knight. His first encounter was with what appeared to him to be huge giants but were in reality windmills. He charged at them with his lance made ready, only to be knocked off his horse by one of the windmill blades. Later, Don Quixote mistakenly thought a cloud of dust made by a flock of sheep to be armies locked in combat. He heroically intervened only to scatter the sheep and be stoned by the angry shepherds. Of course, everyone who came into contact with him considered him a crazy, deluded old man.

Christians are sometimes looked upon in the same way. According to Scripture, Christ inaugurated an ironic kingdom, and believers in Christ are partakers of this kingdom and rule together with their Savior. Christians march throughout their lives as knightly warriors for God's kingdom, and in so doing they reign spiritually over satanic evil. However, the world places no credence in Scripture and looks upon those who do as people caught up in fairy tales and mythical legends. Biblical ideas of demons and Satan are viewed as too absurd for logical minds of the twenty-first century to entertain seriously. It is especially outlandish for Christians to consider themselves knights of Christ battling against unseen forces of spiritual darkness.

Of course, from our present perspective, there is a fundamental difference between the truly deluded Quixote and Christians at the level of reality. The well-known molecular scientist Francis Crick has said that those with religious faith are a part of a "lunatic fringe" and "what everyone believed yesterday, and you believe today, only cranks will believe tomorrow."[22] Christians are seen by some as deluded dreamers, even lunatic types like Don Quixote, who believe they are fighting satanic giants when there are none. Yet, ironically, the unseen reality of Christ's kingdom and of Satan is a spiritual reality, at least according to Scripture's evaluation.

I alluded to the spiritual kingship of believers when discussing Christ's ironic rule in Revelation 2:26–27 and 3:21. The first indication in Revelation of believers' ironic rule on earth is found in 1:5–6. There, in verse 5, Christ is called "ruler of the kings of the earth," and in the latter part of the same verse and in verse 6 it is explained *how* his universal rule is shared with others: Christ loves us and released us from our sins by his blood, and through his death he has made us to be a kingdom, priests to his God. In other words, the end-time kingdom of the Messiah also consists of his followers who coreign with him. As will become evident, the reign of Christian believers as a kingdom and priests is an idea that John mentions not only rarely or occasionally. In fact, Revelation 1:5–6 is repeated virtually verbatim in 5:9–10. Believers exercise their rule in the same way that Jesus did. Jesus was victorious by persevering in his witness to the Father even though he was pressured and tempted to stop doing so. He persisted in this witness and did not compromise even when threatened with death. It is the same with those who follow Christ.

Consequently, Christians exercise their latter-day kingship in the same manner as their Savior. Just as Jesus's witness spiritually conquered Satan at the cross, so Christians' witness overcomes Satan, since it is the means by which unbelievers hear the gospel, believe, and hence are delivered from Satan's bondage. Christians are to reproduce in themselves the witness of Christ, both in word and life-

---

22. Francis Crick, *Of Molecules and Men* (Seattle: University of Washington Press, 1966), 99.

style. They are to live a cruciform life in conformity to their crucified Savior. They also may be tempted to compromise and to take a low profile in this witnessing role, and when they resist temptation to compromise and faithfully persevere, they may suffer and appear defeated in the earthly sphere. Yet as long as they maintain their witness, they are spiritually reigning over Satan in the midst of apparent defeat, just as their Savior did. With Christ, believers also hold power over "the keys of death and of Hades" (Rev. 1:18), as their witness is the catalyst of the Spirit in delivering people from the domain of darkness (Col. 1:13) and tearing off the blindfold with which "the god of this world [Satan] has blinded the minds of the unbelieving" (2 Cor. 4:4).

John himself knew from personal experience what it means to exercise ironic kingly power in Jesus's eschatological kingdom:

> I, John, your brother and fellow partaker in the *tribulation* and *kingdom* and *perseverance* which are in Jesus, was on the island called Patmos because of the word of God and the *testimony of Jesus*. (Rev. 1:9)

Here in John's self-description is found in capsule form a picture of the Christian's end-time kingship, which consists of three essential elements. (1) John had faithfully continued to witness about Jesus through his words and deeds, although he had been strongly pressured to quit giving such a witness. As a result, he suffered *tribulation* by being sentenced to exile on an island. It is probable that one of the ways in which he was tempted to compromise his testimony was by giving some formal, public acknowledgment that Caesar was Lord. Because he would not do so, he suffered apparent social and political defeat. (2) Nevertheless, his *perseverance* in faith and witnessing was evidence that (3) he was spiritually reigning in a *kingdom* with

Christ. It certainly didn't look like John was ruling as a king, but he really was because he was "in Jesus," that is, in union with his Savior, which meant that he would "follow the Lamb" (Rev. 14:4) in whatever ironic suffering path he trod.

However, according to John, for a Christian to be a spiritual king also means that he is a priest (Rev. 1:6; 5:10). Believers are priestly mediators between God and ungodly people as they share their witness to Christ. Consequently, as Christ reigned as a priestly king, so do Christians rule under the ultimate lordship of Christ.

And, as was the case with Christ, so John clearly understands that Christians began to reign in the messianic kingdom after the resurrection and do so throughout the church age until the second coming. Of course, this is an idea quite contrary to that of many evangelical Christians, who believe that both Jesus and Christians do not reign in the messianic kingdom prophesied in the Old Testament until after his second coming. Apparently, for Christians such as Tim LaHaye and Jerry B. Jenkins, like Hal Lindsey, the end times do not begin until the final tribulation and Jesus's final bodily coming.[23]

However, that the New Testament views Jesus and Christians as spiritually ruling in the end times should already be evident from our discussions in this section. That this is also John's understanding becomes discernable from a more in-depth look at Revelation 1. In verses 5, 6, and 11 John speaks of Christ and believers *already* exercising their rule! Furthermore, he sees this ironic dominion as a beginning fulfillment of Daniel's prophecy of the messianic kingdom. For example, in Revelation 1:1 John says that God gave the revelation to John "to show . . . the things which must soon take place."

---

23. See Tim LaHaye's and Jerry B. Jenkins's Left Behind series (12 vols.), which affirms the latter days do not formally begin until the rapture, followed by the great tribulation and Christ's millennial reign, though they believe we are on the verge of these latter days beginning. E.g., see Tim LaHaye and Jerry B. Jenkins, *Left Behind: A Novel of the Earth's Last Days* (Wheaton, IL: Tyndale, 1995).

The latter part of the verse is an allusion to Daniel 2:28,[24] which has already received some study: "God . . . reveals . . . and He has made known . . . what will take place in the latter days."

Daniel 2:28, as we have seen, introduces the prophetic vision of that chapter, which predicts that the Messiah will defeat the evil world kingdom, a visionary theme synonymous with Daniel 7. However, John has made a crucial change in the wording of Daniel 2:28. Instead of reiterating, like Daniel, that the Messiah's defeat will occur in the distant "latter days," he substitutes "soon" for "latter days." That is, the change of wording implies that Daniel's "latter days" (during which a messianic kingdom would be established) are about to be fulfilled in John's own time, if not already beginning to happen.[25] Indeed, the following references to a *past* and *present* reality of the kingdom (vv. 6, 9) and of the "Son of Man's" rule (vv. 7, 13–14) indicate that verse 1 is speaking of an *initial fulfillment* of the messianic prophecies of Daniel 2, which will continue on into the future.[26]

John's perception that Daniel's prophecy has already begun fulfillment may also be evident from verse 3: "for the time is near." John may be using these words as a figurative expression to say that not only is the time of *fulfillment* near, but it is also just beginning to emerge in the present. The phrase has a striking parallel in Mark 1:15, which could confirm the figurative interpretation of Revelation

---

24. The allusion is probably drawn from the Greek version of the Old Testament (the Old Greek or Theodotion version of the Greek OT). In addition to Dan. 2:28, the allusion could come also from 2:29, 45, since they are almost identical in phraseology.

25. Interpreters such as John Walvoord, *The Revelation of Jesus Christ* (London: Marshall, Morgan, & Scott, 1966), 35, understand "soon" as referring to the speedy manner in which the fulfillment of the Old Testament prophecies is to occur and not to the time when such prophecies will take place. However, the phrase *en tachei* ("soon" or "quickly") must refer to the time of fulfillment as imminent or already in process, since "soon" is substituted for Daniel's "in the latter days," which obviously concerns the temporal aspect of prophetic realization rather than the manner.

26. If John sees Daniel's prophecy as beginning fulfillment, it would not be unique in the New Testament, since Luke 20:18 (Matt. 21:44) identifies the prophesied "stone" of Dan. 2:34–35 with Christ and reaching fulfillment in him. For a more detailed discussion of John's understanding of Dan. 2:28–29, 45, see my article "Influence of Daniel upon the Structure and Theology of John's Apocalypse."

1:3. Jesus announces here, "The time is fulfilled and the kingdom of God has drawn near" (my translation). The second phrase concerning the kingdom having drawn near is probably a further figurative way to say that the time of the Old Testament messianic prophecies is being fulfilled. So also the expression of nearness in Revelation 1:3 may have the same figurative idea, denoting "present time." Perhaps it is no coincidence that prominent scholars have seen the words in the second phrase of Mark 1:15 as Jesus's way of claiming that the prophecies of Daniel had started their fulfillment in his earthly ministry. In particular, Jesus's words "The kingdom of God is at hand" have been viewed as an allusion to the prophecy in Daniel 7:22: "The *time arrived* when the saints took possession of *the kingdom*."[27] Consequently, Christ believed this kingdom was being established in his own lifetime. Likewise, Revelation 1:3 is probably alluding to Daniel 7:22 to signify the same thing. The very least that can be said is that John saw the inaugurated fulfillment of Daniel's prophecies about the end times beginning to happen in his own lifetime.

Another Dimension of the Saints' End-Time Kingdom

If it is true that Christians ironically reign on earth through their sufferings while being led by their heavenly Lord, what happens when a Christian dies? John answers this question in Revelation 2:10–11:

> Do not fear what you are about to suffer. Behold, the devil is about to cast some of you into prison, so that you will be tested, and you will have tribulation for ten days. *Be faithful until death*, and I will give you the crown of life. . . . He who overcomes will not be hurt by the second death.

---

27. So F. F. Bruce, *New Testament Development of Old Testament Themes* (Grand Rapids, MI: Eerdmans, 1970), 23–30; C. H. Dodd, *According to the Scriptures: The Sub-Structure of New Testament Theology* (New York: Scribner, 1953), 69.

Upon death the believer's soul is resurrected to heaven, and he joins Christ and reigns together with him on his throne. The ultimate irony of the saints' end-time reign with Jesus is that when they experience *physical death* and apparent *defeat* because of their faith, they are given spiritual *life* and a *victor's crown*. The end of their physical existence is the beginning of a spiritual existence with the heavenly Lord. In this they follow the same ironic pattern of their Lord's death, which led to resurrected life. Therefore, believers who so conquer their physical death cannot be hurt by the second death, which is eternal separation from God. However, all unbelievers will suffer the first and second death.

The same ironic picture is painted by John in Revelation 20:4 and 6, where dead saints are seen as reigning with Christ in heaven:

> I saw the souls of those who had been beheaded because of their testimony of Jesus . . . and those who had not worshiped the beast or his image . . . and they came to life and reigned with Christ [in heaven]. . . . Blessed and holy is the one who has a part in the first resurrection; over these the second death has no power, but they will be priests of God . . . and will reign with Him.[28]

Thus the end-time reign of believers with Christ especially reaches its zenith at the end time of their lives when they suffer the physical defeat of death, which is turned into the victory of spiritual eternal life, which will be consummated at the very end of time in a perfected spiritual and physical resurrection.

---

28. We are not concerned here to discuss the thorny problem of the meaning of the "thousand years" during which the saints are said to reign. Whatever time period is in mind, the ironic principle of death being transformed into life is involved. Nevertheless, the idea of Rev. 20:4–6 is probably the same as that of 2:10–11.

The Various Ways We Reign with
Christ in Day-to-Day Living

What are the different ways in which Christians exercise their rule with Christ in these "latter days"? Of course, one of the most overt ways is to suffer death for the sake of one's faith. Throughout the course of the church age, there have been Christians, like Stephen in Acts 7, who follow Christ's life pattern: persevering through faith in the midst of pressures to compromise and being killed as a result. Many have so sacrificed their lives for the sake of the spread of the gospel. They have spiritually conquered by allowing themselves to be conquered by bodily death.

However, to one degree or another all Christians are faced with the challenge of persevering through temptations to compromise their faith. Like Christ, believers will suffer and be defeated in numerous areas of life, but if they continue to trust God during their trials, they will be spiritual conquerors. As Jesus said, "If any one wishes to come after Me, he must deny himself, and take up his cross and follow Me" (Matt. 16:24). The apostle John endured political and social defeat in exile on the isle of Patmos. However, he was a conqueror, reigning in Jesus's invisible messianic kingdom because he kept his faith.

Some of the Christians in Smyrna and Thyatira underwent economic deprivation due to their Christian witness. In these Asia Minor cities, the major businesses or trades had organized trade unions or guilds (e.g., silversmiths, dyers of linens). Usually these unions had annual conventions or trade-union meetings in pagan temples, which all in a particular trade were expected to attend. One of the main activities at these annual meetings was to worship the idol-god who was supposedly responsible for protecting the economic prosperity of the trade. Often such worship was expressed through eating a meal dedicated to the guardian deity. Christians in Smyrna and Thyatira would not attend such meetings, since it would have compromised their Christian testimony. Consequently, they were excluded from union membership. Such exclusion, in essence, meant they could not practice their trade, since no one else would carry on business with them. Against this background, John's description of believers in Smyrna should be more appreciated: "I know your tribulation and your poverty (but you are rich)" (Rev. 2:9). They were financially poor because they were rich in faith. They conquered spiritually by being economically conquered, and by persisting in faith they were reigning with Christ in the end-time kingdom (see likewise Rom. 8:35–37).

How should Christians in business today respond when their competitors are making huge profits through various unethical practices? Certainly they would be tempted to do likewise. But they spiritually overcome when they continue to maintain Christian integrity, while being overcome or suffering economically. When Christians exhibit such faithfulness in business dealings, they are exercising their eschatological and spiritual rule with Christ.

Paul refers to a similar idea in Romans 12:1, when he exhorts believers: "Present your bodies a living and holy sacrifice, acceptable to God, which is your spiritual service of worship." We are to sacrifice ourselves when we experience some setback on the earthly level. And when we do, we win a spiritual victory in the same manner as did Christ. To cite a mundane example, let us say that a husband and wife radically disagree about what kind of house they should buy. Sometimes one of them must sacrifice their ego and have their preference defeated, while believing, nevertheless, that God will work the circumstances together for the good of the marriage (Paul says that husbands should be the ones so to sacrifice, Eph. 5:25).

Such belief conquers apparent psychological defeat in interpersonal relationships.

How do you react when you are offended by friends or business associates? Do you feel you must get back at them in some way, perhaps at least to the extent of ignoring them? Or perhaps you feel you must say something to them that will make them feel bad. Paul's exhortation to sacrifice in Romans 12:1 is further explained by this general kind of personal conflict that Paul has in mind in Romans 12:17, 21:

> Never pay back evil for evil to anyone. . . . Do not be overcome
> by evil, but overcome evil with good.

When we are wronged and trampled underfoot in daily interpersonal relationships, we conquer with the self-sacrifice of refusing to seek revenge. To the degree that Christians practice such self-sacrifice, ironically they exercise their end-time messianic reign in the kingdom with Christ. Jesus's end-time kingdom is not reserved only for some far-off (or near) day, when he returns a second time! No, it is going on right now where we live.

Conclusion

What Irony Is Being Played Out in Your Life?

Regardless of who we are, whether believers in Christ or unbelievers, an irony is being played out in our life. If we are unbelievers, then in one way or another and at some point in our life, we will suffer retributive irony; that is, we will be punished by means of our own sin. On the other hand, if we are Christians, in one way or another, and at some point in our lives, we will experience restorative irony.

Though believers may seem defeated or appear as failures or on the verge of death, God will bless them in the midst of their suffering, if they persevere in faith. When believers are facing apparently sure defeat or suffering, they must trust that God will bring victory through defeat, and strength through weakness, whether in this world or most certainly in the next. Without this kind of irony faith cannot grow. This is why God always at some point in the life of Christians brings impossible or difficult situations to confront them.

The reason that everyone experiences either retributive irony or restorative irony is that they are identified ultimately with either the devil or Christ. Satan experienced judgmental irony when he tried to defeat Christ at the cross. However, as we have seen, Satan himself suffered defeat through Christ's resurrection, by which Christ overcame the penalty and bonds of death in which Satan was attempting to hold him. But even before the resurrection, at the cross, Christ not only *defeated* Satan but defeated him in the midst of his own suffering and defeat. By suffering the penalty of other people's sin on the cross, Christ was at that very time defeating the devil by delivering those for whom he suffered from captivity to the devil. Thus, the very way by which the devil designed to defeat Christ was the very way by which the devil himself was defeated.

Accordingly, all who do not trust in and identify with Christ must identify with Satan and his kingdom. This also means such people identify with the ironic pattern of the devil's destiny. They, like him, may appear to be victorious in this life, even in oppressing the saints. But in reality, their apparent victory and strength are frustrated by God wherein their spiritual defeat begins in the midst of their apparent worldly success or in the midst of their successful oppression of believers. They experience the irony of judgment.

Likewise, yet in contrast, true believers are like their representative Jesus Christ. The restorative irony displayed in Christ's suffering life and death is also displayed in their lives because they are being conformed to Christ's image (Rom. 8:29); that is, they live a cruciform life whereby their faith in the midst of their suffering indicates that they are winning spiritual victory in the midst of their seeming defeat. Such faith indicates that they are actually spiritually strong and on the road to ultimate victory, both spiritually and physically, in the new heavens and new earth.

Revelation 13:16–14:1 depicts the two kinds of people in the world and the character and destiny of each:

He [the second beast of Revelation 13] causes all, the small and the great, and the rich and the poor, and the free men and the slaves, to be given a mark on their right hand or on their forehead, and he provides that no one will be able to buy or to sell, except the one who has the mark, either the name of the [first] beast or the number of his name. Here is wisdom. Let him who has understanding calculate the number of the beast, for the number is that of a man; and his number is six hundred and sixty-six.

Then I looked, and behold, the Lamb was standing on Mount Zion, and with Him one hundred and forty-four thousand, having His name and the name of His Father written on their foreheads.

The first beast represents the unbelieving state, which was Rome in the first century AD. This first beast is a representative of Satan on earth, who does Satan's bidding (see Rev. 13:1–8). The second beast is the PR man for the first beast and probably represents local authorities, such as in first-century Asia Minor. This beast does all he can to get people to believe in, worship, and obey the first beast (see Rev. 13:11–18). Revelation 13:16–14:1 is about unbelievers taking on the character of their dark prince.[1] In this respect, unbelievers are portrayed as receiving "a mark on their right hand or on their forehead" (Rev. 13:16), which is explained as "the name of the [first] beast or the number of his name" (13:17). This beast, as we have seen, is the earthly agent and representative of the dragon, Satan (see Rev. 13:1–3). This mark on the unbeliever is invisible, since the counterpart name on the true believer is invisible (God's people had Christ's name and the name of the Father written on their foreheads 14:1), which is evidence that the two have a parallel spiritual nature and are intended to be compared and contrasted.

---

1. The remainder of this chapter is based for the most part on a revision of G. K. Beale, *We Become What We Worship* (Downers Grove, IL: InterVarsity, 2008), 255–56, 261–62.

Those who have believed in Jesus have been identified with him and his character and are protected against ultimate deception by the power of his name, which is none other than his very presence with them (as 22:4 makes explicit). Their refusal to identify with the beast will result in suffering and even death, but they will have the ultimate reward of eternal life (so 20:4) and are even beginning now ironically to gain victory and receive that reward by enduring through suffering in their faith (so see Rev. 13:11).

Those not trusting in Christ are identified with the beast, lie under the devil's power, are unable to avoid being deceived by the beast (see further on 2:17), and will suffer perdition with the beast (see 14:9–11; 17:11; 19:19–20; and 21:8). They are even now beginning to suffer eternal death in that they are already separated from God's presence, and that is the essence of spiritual death. While identification with the beast gives them temporary prosperity in this life, they are punished ultimately with eternal death (14:9–11).[2] In addition to considering the contrasting "name" in Revelation 14:1, that the mark of the name is figurative and not literal is evident from the first beast, who has written upon his heads blasphemous names, which figuratively connote false claims to earthly, divine kingship (see 13:1).[3] Likewise, the point of saying that the worshipers of the beast have his name written on their head is to underscore the fact that they are identified with him, his character, and his final terrible destiny (e.g., see Rev. 17:8).

The identification of the beast and his followers with 666 in 13:18 indicates the old, imperfect earthly character of the beast's followers. This is not the place to present all the identifications and interpretations of the number 666,[4] but what I have concluded elsewhere as the

---

2. See further discussion on 14:9–11 in G. K. Beale, *Revelation* (Grand Rapids, MI: Eerdmans, 1998), in loc cit.

3. See further discussion on 13:1 in Beale, *Revelation*, in loc cit.

4. Though I have done this elsewhere: see Beale, *Revelation*, in loc cit.

most plausible approach[5] will be laid out here in terms of how it bears upon our present discussion. A common line of interpretation of the meaning of 666 is that of gematria. In the ancient world, letters of the alphabet (in Hebrew, Greek, or Latin) were substituted for numbers (our numerical system derives from later Arabic mathematicians). Therefore, each letter stood for a number. The problem with this is that no clear identification can be made linking 666 with any specific ancient (or modern) name. Attempts have been made to incorporate titles and alter spellings to try to make a multitude of names fit, but nothing conclusive has emerged from this.[6] That the number is not to be understood by means of a literal calculative rendering of someone's name is apparent from the earlier observation that the saints have Christ's and God's name written on their forehead, in the immediately following vision, which is intended as the contrast to 666 in 13:18. Since the former clearly pertains to spiritual realities, this is likely the focus with the latter.

The number seven refers to completeness and is repeated throughout the book.[7] However, 666 appears only in 13:18. This suggests that the triple sixes are intended as a contrast with the divine sevens throughout the book and signify incompleteness and imperfection. Furthermore, if the number of 144,000 saints in the following verse has the figurative force of signifying the complete number of God's people in Christ (see Rev. 14:1), then the intentional contrast with the 666 in the preceding verse would refer to the beast and his people as inherently incomplete. This idea of six is enhanced by observing that the sixth seal, sixth trumpet, and sixth bowl all picture judgment of the beast's followers. The seventh in each series pictures the consummation of the judgments. These three series of seals,

---

5. Beale, *Revelation*, in loc cit.
6. On this see Beale, *Revelation: A Shorter Commentary* (Grand Rapids, MI: Eerdmans, 2015), 284.
7. On this figurative significance of "seven" in Revelation, see Beale, *Revelation*, 58–62.

trumpets, and bowls are incomplete without the seventh.[8] While the beast and his followers strive to be complete in and of themselves, they can never achieve seven, the number of completeness in Christ.

The number three in the Bible signifies completeness, as, for example, is expressed by the completeness of the Godhead in Revelation 1:4–5, which is parodied by the dragon, beast, and false prophet here in Revelation 13 (and in 16:13).[9] Therefore, the repetition of "six" three times indicates the completeness of sinful incompleteness found in the beast. The beast ironically epitomizes imperfection, while striving to achieve his own purported divine perfection. Three sixes are a parody of the divine Trinity of three sevens; that is, though the beast attempts to mimic God, Christ, and the prophetic Spirit of truth (19:10), no matter how hard he tries, he cannot but fall short of succeeding. He cannot successfully complete his attempts perfectly to image God and exalt himself above God. The reason for using sixes instead of sevens to describe the beast in verse 18 is that of the repeated emphasis in Revelation 13:3–14 upon the beast as a counterfeit Christ or prophet.

Though the satanic beasts appear successfully to imitate the true and righteous God in their attempts to deceive, ironically they remain thoroughly evil on the inside and fall far short of the divine character they are mimicking. So also their followers become evil and fall short of the divine character but imitate the satanic character of those they revere. No matter how hard they try to find completeness outside of Christ, ironically they find only incompleteness.

The phrase in Revelation 13:18, "for the number is that of a man," could be translated as, "for the number is that of a [specific] man." But it is better to translate it generically as, "for the number is of human-

---

8. E. Boring, *Revelation* (Louisville, KY: John Knox, 1989), 162–63.
9. Cf. further J. F. Drinkard, "Numbers," in *Harper's Bible Dictionary*, ed. P. J. Achetemeier (San Francisco: Harper & Row, 1985), 711–12.

ity." This Greek word for *man* is often generic when it occurs without an article, as here and in 21:17, where the "measurement of a man" (the literal Greek phrase) means a "human measurement" (using the same Greek word for *man* as in Rev. 13:18). Likewise, the omission of the definite article in 13:18 suggests the general idea of humanity, not some special individual who can be discerned only through an esoteric manner of calculation. It is a number common to fallen humanity, which identifies with the beast, the emissary of Satan.

Thus, the number in Revelation 13:18 is that of incomplete humanity apart from Christ. The beast is the supreme representative of unregenerate humanity, separated from God and unable to achieve divine likeness but always trying. Humanity was created on the sixth day, but without the seventh day of rest Adam and Eve would have been imperfect and incomplete, a rest they never fully inherited. The triple-six figures emphasize that the beast and his followers try to find perfection and ultimate rest but despite all their efforts fall short of God's creative purposes for humanity.

Thus, "there is a way which seems right to a man, but its end is the way of death" (Prov. 14:12; 16:25). Their striving for completeness without Christ leads ironically only to their spiritual incompleteness in this life and the next and even physical incompleteness at the final judgment, when they will experience the resurrection to death (see John 5:28–29; Rev. 20:12–15; 21:8). Even "good" people are caught in this ironic web of vain striving, since though "good," they are without Christ.

May the Lord cause us to strive to achieve the seven of completeness in him rather than the wind of attempted completeness outside of him. Such people will find only ultimate incompleteness and that his number—666—is up.

General Index

Scripture Index

Short Studies in Biblical Theology Series

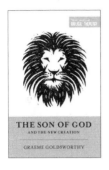

THE SON OF GOD
AND THE NEW CREATION

GRAEME GOLDSWORTHY

MARRIAGE
AND THE MYSTERY OF THE GOSPEL

RAY ORTLUND

WORK
AND OUR LABOR IN THE LORD

JAMES M. HAMILTON JR.

COVENANT
AND GOD'S PURPOSE FOR THE WORLD

THOMAS R. SCHREINER

THE CITY OF GOD
AND THE GOAL OF CREATION

T. DESMOND ALEXANDER

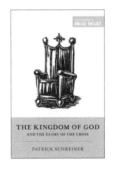

THE KINGDOM OF GOD
AND THE GLORY OF THE CROSS

PATRICK SCHREINER

FROM CHAOS TO COSMOS
CREATION TO NEW CREATION

SIDNEY GREIDANUS

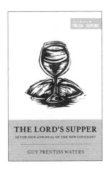

THE LORD'S SUPPER
AS THE SIGN AND SEAL OF THE NEW COVENANT

GUY PRENTISS WATERS

REDEMPTIVE REVERSALS
AND THE IRONIC OVERTURNING OF HUMAN WISDOM

G. K. BEALE

For more information, visit **crossway.org/ssbt**.